DRAMA START

Drama Activities, Plays and Monologues for Young Children (Ages 3-8)

First published in 2011 by
JemBooks
Montenotte,
Cork,
Ireland
www.jembooks.ie

ISBN: 978-0-9568966-0-5

Cover design by Jer Macauliffe
Typesetting by Gough Typesetting Service, Dublin

DRAMA START

DRAMA ACTIVITIES, PLAYS AND MONOLOGUES FOR YOUNG CHILDREN (AGES 3-8)

Julie Meighan

JemBooks

About the Author

Julie Meighan is a lecturer in Drama in Education at the Cork Institute of Technology. She has taught Drama to all age groups and levels. She is the author of "Drama Start".

Contents

PART ONE: DRAMA GAMES

Warm-Up Games

Co-operative Games

Listening Games

Observation Games

Communication Games

Concentration Games

Movement Games

Contents

Role Playing Games

Action Poems

PART TWO: CHILDREN'S PLAYS

PART THREE: MONOLOGUES FOR CHILDREN

Monologues for Children (Girls)

Monologues for Children (Boys)

'Drama Start' is a collection of drama activities, including games, role playing ideas, action poems, plays and monologues, suitable for children between the ages of three and eight. It can be used in Early Years' settings or in primary schools, up to and including second class. This book is also suitable for people working with children in any setting where drama is used, such as community groups, out of school care facilities, therapeutic group work and so on.

The book is accessible and easy to follow. It is divided into three parts:

Part 1 – Drama Games
Part 2 – Plays
Part 3 – Monologues

Each section provides educators/teachers/leaders with a variety of creative and imaginative ideas to stimulate drama activities, in many different settings.

Part One: Drama Games

There are nine different categories in this section, including warm-up games, listening games, observation games and so on. Within each category, the main benefit of the featured games is stated. Some of the games may have more than one benefit. For example, the game 'Fruit Basket' is listed in the warm-up games' section but playing it also has other benefits, such as developing listening and observation skills.

The games are clearly set out and the appropriate age group and minimum amount of children needed to participate are listed for each one. Detailed instructions are also provided, with suggested variations for some of the games.

Warm-Up Games

These games can be used at the beginning of any drama lesson. They help to limber the children up and to get them ready for the next part of the lesson. The warm-up games below are fun and enjoyable.

If you are short on time the children can also do them by themselves, in separate groups.

Game: Magic Rocks
Age: 3 years+
Minimum number of participants: 2
Resources needed: Clear space, a wand (optional).
Other Benefits: To stimulate children's imagination and creativity.
Instructions: Get each child to find a clear space. They must make sure that they are not touching anyone else. The children crouch down on the floor and make a ball shape with their bodies. The teacher explains that all children are magic rocks and that the teacher is a magic wizard. The teacher waves the magic wand and says: "Magic rocks turn into dinosaurs." All the children turn into dinosaurs and move around the room as dinosaurs. The teacher then says: "Magic rocks turn into magic rocks." The children return to their clear spaces and crouch down on the floor again as quickly as possible.

The magic wizard can change the magic rocks into anything they want, for example superheroes, animals, people, household items and so on.
Variation: The children can take it turns to be the magic wizard.

Game: Octopus
Age: 4 years+
Minimum number of participants: 3
Resources needed: Clear space.
Other Benefits: This game can be used to work on co-operation and teamwork skills.
Instructions: One child is chosen or volunteers to be the octopus and stands in the middle of the clear space. The rest of the children should line up along one side of the space. When the octopus shouts out "Octopus!" the other children have to run past the octopus and try to reach the other side without being caught. Children that are caught become part of the octopus's arms. They are not allowed to let go of each other's hands. Only the children at the ends of the octopus's arms can catch people.

As the game progresses, the octopus becomes longer and longer. The game becomes more difficult, as more and more children become part of the octopus's arms. It ends when all the children are caught.

Game: Prison Break
Age: 4 years+
Minimum number of participants: 3
Resources needed: Clear space.
Other Benefits: This is a warm up game that children really enjoy. It also can be used to improve listening and co-ordination skills.
Instructions: Children all line up on one side of the clear space. One student is chosen, or volunteers, to be the guard on duty and stands in the centre of the room. The rest of the children are prisoners. When the guard shouts out "Prison break!" all the prisoners must run to the other side of the space. If the guard catches a prisoner they also become a guard.

Eventually there will be more guards then prisoners. The last prisoner becomes the first guard on duty for the next game.

Game: Fruit Basket
Age: 4 years+
Minimum number of participants: 7
Resources needed: Clear space and a chair for each student – if you do not have chairs you can use sheets of paper or cushions.
Other Benefits: This is a well-known game which can also be used very effectively as a listening game or as an observation game.
Instructions: All the children sit in circle on a chair or a cushion. The teacher chooses three different fruits and goes around the circle giving each person the name of a fruit, in a particular order, for example, apple, orange, banana. A child is then chosen, or volunteers, to go into the centre of the circle. His/Her chair is taken away.

The child in the centre calls out the name of one of the three fruits. If the child in the centre says apple then all the apples change place, if s/he says banana, all the bananas change place and if s/he says orange, all the oranges change places. If s/he says fruit basket then everyone changes places. The child who is left without a chair goes into the centre for the next round.
Variations: There are lots of variations to this game and you can change the names to go with a specific theme. Fruit basket – apple, orange, and banana –could be replaced by:

Barnyard – chicken, pig and cow.
Zoo – elephant, giraffe and tiger.
Circus – clown, ringmaster and acrobat
Ocean – fish, mermaid and shark.

Game: Crossing the circle
Age: 5 years+
Minimum number of participants: 6
Resources: Clear space.
Other Benefits: This game can be difficult at first but it an excellent way to get the children to use their imagination and creativity.
Instructions: All the children stand in a circle and the teacher gives them a number, 1, 2 or 3. The teacher then calls out a number, for example "3". Everyone in the circle who has been given number 3 must cross the circle and swap places with someone else who has the same number.

Once the children have got used to crossing the circle, the teacher calls out a number and a way of moving, such as walking, running, hopping, crawling, twirling, dancing, slow motion, zig-zag and so on.
Variation: This activity can also be used for older children. The children can cross the circle in a role. For example, the teacher calls out a number and a character, such as a ballerina, an artist, a lion, a model, an astronaut, a duck, someone who is stuck in mud, a toddler who has just begun to walk, someone walking on hot sand or someone splashing in puddles.

Game: What's the time Mr. Wolf?
Age: 3 years+
Minimum number of participants: 4
Requirements: Clear space.
Other Benefits: This is a popular traditional children's game that can also be used very effectively in a drama session as a warm-up game. This game also helps children with their listening and co-ordination skills.
Instructions: One child is chosen or volunteers to be Mr. or Ms. Wolf and stands at one side of the clear space. His/Her back is to the other children, who are standing at the opposite end of the space. The rest of the children shout out: "What's the time Mr. /Ms. Wolf?" The Wolf does not turn around. He/she replies in a rough, wolf-like voice: "four o'clock." The children walk forward the number of steps the wolf calls out (in this case, four). The children ask again: "What time is it Mr./Ms. Wolf?" The wolf replies: "five o'clock." The children take five steps forward.

The children continue to ask the question and to walk the appropriate amount of steps forward. Eventually, when the wolf thinks that the children are near enough he/she will say: "Dinnertime!" Then the wolf turns around and chases the children. They have to try to rush back to their starting place. If Mr./Ms. Wolf catches one of them before they reach home, that child is the wolf in the next game.

Game: Pppppppopcorn
Age: 4 years+
Minimum number of participants: 3
Resources needed: Clear space.
Other Benefits: This game also helps with observation and co-ordination skills.
Instructions: Everybody is in a circle. The children crouch down on the floor. Each child takes a turn jumping up and down, saying "pop" or making a popping sound that sounds like popcorn popping.

The children take turns in order but if two children jump up and pop at the same time, they are out of the game. Each round can be faster than the last round.

Game: The Name Game
Age: 3 years+
Minimum number of participants: 2
Resources needed: Clear space.
Other Benefits: This is an excellent way for children to get to know each other's names and it helps them to become part of a group.
Instructions: All the children stand in a circle. The teacher has a small ball in his/her hand. The teacher asks one child to say their name, and then the teacher gently throws the ball to that child. The child replies, using the teacher's name, for example: "Thank you, Miss Brophy!" and throws back the ball. The teacher responds using the child's name, for example: says, "You're welcome Anna!"

The teacher continues to gently throw the ball to each child around the circle and they throw it back. Once a child has tossed the ball to the teacher they must put their hands behind their back to stop it been thrown to them again. The teacher needs to make sure that every child has received the ball and said their name. The game ends when the last child throws the ball back to the teacher.

Game: Crocodile, Crocodile may we cross the river?
Age: 4 years+
Minimum number of participants: 3
Resources needed: Clear space.
Other Benefits: This is another popular and traditional game that works very well as a drama warm-up activity.
Instructions: In the centre of the clear space set an area as the river, with a river bank on either side. Masking tape or chairs can be used to make the demarcation. One child is chosen or volunteers to be the crocodile. The crocodile stands in the middle of the river and the rest of the children stand on one bank of the river.

The children on the bank all chant together: "Please, Crocodile, Crocodile may we cross your golden river?" Crocodile replies with a condition, for example: "Yes if you have black hair," or "Yes if you have a brother," or "Yes if you are wearing red." Children who fulfil the condition may cross unchallenged. The rest have to try to get across without being caught. If they are caught they are out. The game continues until there are no more children left to catch. The last child caught becomes the crocodile.

Game: Sharks and Islands
Age: 4 years+
Minimum number of participants: 6
Resources needed: Clear space, a newspaper.
Other Benefits: This is a very popular warm-up game. It also helps children with both their co-ordination and reaction skills.

Instructions: Divide up the newspaper and spread the sheets out around the clear space. The newspapers are islands and the rest of the space is the water. The teacher is the shark and the children are swimmers. The swimmers start swimming around the space. When the teacher shouts out: "SHARK ATTACK!" the swimmers must get onto an island. The objective is for the shark to catch any swimmers who are not standing completely on an island. Even if just their toe is off the island they become sharks.

After each shark attack, the sharks tear a piece off each newspaper sheet so the islands gradually become smaller. This continues until all the swimmers have become sharks.

Game: Sleeping! Sleeping!
Age: 3 years+
Minimum number of participants: 2
Resources needed: Clear space.
Other Benefits: Stimulates the children's imaginations and helps with their sense of movement.
Instructions: The teacher gets all the children to stretch and yawn and then they lie down on the floor. Tell them that they are going to sleep. Get them to snore very loudly. The teacher says very softly: "dreaming, dreaming, all the children are dreaming and in their dreams they are a prince/princess." Then all the children get up and become a prince/princess.

They can dream that they are both people and objects. For example, rocking chairs, dinosaurs, mice, runners, superheroes, computers, ballerinas, astronauts and so on.

Game: Red Rover
Age: 4 years+
Minimum number of participants: 6
Resources needed: Clear space.
Other Benefits: This is a very good warm-up game and it also helps the children to work as part of a team.
Instructions: The class is divided into two groups. Each group hold hands and the two groups form a line facing each other. One side starts by picking a person on the opposing team, for example Adam, and saying: "Red Rover, Red Rover, send Adam over." Adam then lets go of his team-mates' hands and runs towards the other line. His aim is to break through it. If Adam breaks through, he chooses one person from that team to join his team, and they both walk back and join his line. If Adam fails to break through, he becomes part of the other team. Each team alternates calling children over, until one team has all the people and is declared the winner.

Co-operative Games

The co-operative games below help children to learn how to work together and become part of a group. They help the children to trust one another.

The games are very useful in helping to build a child's self-confidence and raise their self-esteem. Children also discover how satisfactory it can be to be a part of group.

Game: Ten to One
Age: 5 years+
Minimum number of participants: 5
Resources needed: Clear space.
Other Benefits: The children work as part as a group to reach a goal. It is also an excellent game to use to improve reactions and it helps to develop eye contact.
Instructions: The group sits in a circle. Get the children to count from one to ten together. Then children have to count to ten, with one child saying one number at a time. One child volunteers to start counting. Any of the children can say the next number, however, the count stops if two or more children speak at the same time. Then the children have to restart the count. If everyone works together as a team the group can reach ten very quickly. Older children can try this game by counting in reverse from ten to one.

Game: Master and Robots
Age: 5 years+
Minimum number of participants: 2
Resources needed: Clear space.
Other Benefits: The children work as part of a pair but it helps them practise giving clear directions to their partners.
Instructions: This is a fun game that children really enjoy. Divide the group into pairs. Child A is the master and child B is the robot. The master must guide the robot around the clear space by giving them very specific directions. The masters can say for example: "go ten steps forwards" or "put your hands in the air and turn around five times". The masters must make sure that their robot does not bump into other masters and robots in the group.

Game: Machines
Age: 5 years+
Minimum number of participants: 4
Resources needed: Clear space.
Other Benefits: The children experience working as part of a small group and they also get to be creative.
Instructions: Divide the class into groups of four. The teacher calls out the name of a machine. The groups of four use their bodies to make the machines. Each child is a different part of the machine for example, washing machine, popcorn-maker, computer, photocopier, toaster, aeroplane, coffee maker and train. The teacher can ask the children to call out suggestions for machines they would like to make.

Game: Alien, Cow and Tiger
Age: 5 years+
Minimum number of participants: 3
Resources needed: Clear space.
Other Benefits: This game is also an excellent listening game.
Instructions: The teacher shows the children the following actions:

> An alien – the children hold both middle fingers beside their heads and say: "Nanu Nanu."

> A cow – the children bend forward hold their right hands on their stomachs and say: "Moooo."

> A tiger – the children push their right hands forward, imitating a claw and roar.

When the teacher counts to three, each child must choose to be an alien, a cow or a tiger. The objective of the game is for everyone to do the same action. This will not happen at first but if the children work as a team they should manage to be in sync with one another in the end.

Game: Caterpillar
Age: 4 years+
Minimum number of participants: 4
Resources needed: Clear space.
Other Benefits: This game gets the children to work together but it is also very good for improving co-ordination skills.
Instructions: The children lie on their stomachs, side-to-side, with their arms straight out in front of them. The child on the end begins to roll over the top of the row of bodies until he or she gets to the end. Each child gets an opportunity to roll over the row of bodies until they reach the end.

Game: Balloons
Age: 5 years+
Minimum number of participants: 4
Resources needed: Clear space, balloons.
Other Benefits: An excellent team work game – fun and enjoyable.
Instructions: Divide the class into groups of four. Each group gets a balloon. They must work together to keep their balloon up in the air. The balloon mustn't touch the ground. The teacher can make it more difficult for older children. For example they must keep their hands behind their back, kneel on the ground or move only by hopping on one leg.

Game: Co-operative Musical Chairs
Age: 4 years+
Minimum number of participants: 5
Resources needed: Clear space, chairs, CD player, music.
Other Benefits: This is an excellent movement and group game. It promotes problem solving as well as co-operation.
Instructions: Everyone sits on a chair. The music starts and the children all move around while the teacher removes one chair. When the music stops everyone needs to find a chair. The children have to work together and co-operate in order to find room for everyone. This may mean sitting on laps and sharing chairs. After each round a chair is removed but no one is eliminated.

Game: Dragon's Tail
Age: 7 years+
Minimum number of participants: 6
Resources needed: Clear space.
Other Benefits: A great game for developing a sense of teamwork.
Instructions: All the children form one long line, holding on to the child in front of them by the waist. The child at the top of the line becomes the dragon's head. The child in the rear is the dragon's tail. All the other children are the dragon's body and must work as a team to stay connected. The main objective is for the tail to catch the head while keeping the dragon's body intact.

Game: Crows and Cranes
Age: 5 years+
Minimum number of participants: 10
Resources needed: Clear space.
Other Benefits: This can also be a very useful listening game.
Instructions: Divide the children into two groups. One group is called the crows and the other is called the cranes. When the teacher shouts out "crows" all the crows have to chase the cranes. If a crane is caught he/she becomes a crow. When the teacher shouts out "cranes" all the cranes must catch the crows. The game ends when the crows have captured all the cranes or vice versa.

Listening Games

The games below promote active listening among young children and good listening skills improve both attention and concentration. The games help children to learn how to follow instructions and directions. They also make children aware of the importance of listening to what other people have to say.

Game: Traffic Lights
Age: 3 years+
Minimum number of participants: 3
Resources needed: Clear space, something to represent the colours of traffic lights – red, amber, green.
Other Benefits: This is a fun game which young children love. It is also a very good activity to help develop both listening and co-ordination skills.
Instructions: Before the game begins the teacher shows the children a set of traffic lights or the colours in a set of traffic lights. The teacher asks them what the different colours mean and explains that red means stop, amber means prepare to stop and green means go. Then get the children to imagine they are different forms of transport such as bikes, cars, lorries, motorbikes, trucks, scooters, and skateboards. The children then move around the room pretending to be their chosen mode of transport. The teacher can either hold up the traffic light colour and not say anything or shout out the colour and the children must do the following:

"Green" – walk/run around the space.
"Amber" – walk in slow motion.
"Red" – stop and stand still or lie down on the ground!

The teacher calls out the traffic light colours in a mixed-up order. If the children do the wrong action they are out. The last child still left in the game takes over from the teacher and calls out the colours of the traffic lights in the next round.

Game: Animals, animals where are you?
Age: 5 years+
Minimum number of participants: 6
Resources needed: Clear space, pictures of various animals.
Other Benefits: This is an energetic and chaotic game which is very good for improving a child's ability to work in a team.
Instructions: Give each child a picture of an animal such as a cat, a dog, a lion, an elephant and so on. There must be at least two pictures of each animal. The children must move around the clear space, making the sound of the animal in their picture. They cannot tell anyone what animal they are. The objective of this game is for the children to listen carefully to all the animal noises and to form a group with the animals who makes the same noise they do.

Game: Reverse the Car
Age: 3 years+
Minimum number of participants: 5
Resources: Clear space, a toy car.
Other Benefits: This game encourages children to react quickly.
Instructions: This is a good listening game which is fun and always leads to a lot of confusion. The children sit/stand in a circle. A toy car is passed around the circle. The teacher shouts out reverse, the car has to change direction. When the children are comfortable with the car changing directions a second car can be introduced to the circle and then any child can shout out reverse.

Game: Swap Places
Age: 5 years+
Minimum number of participants: 4
Resources: Clear space, chairs or cushions.
Other Benefits: This game encourages the children to use their imaginations and have fun.
Instructions: This game is similar to 'Fruit Basket' and can also be used as a warm-up. Everyone sits on a chair/cushion in a circle. Choose a child to stand in the middle and take away his/her chair. S/he (or the teacher) calls out: "Everyone swaps seats who… for example is wearing a watch, supports Manchester United, has red hair, is wearing socks, likes sweets and so on.

No one can change places with the person sitting next to them. The child in the middle needs to find a seat. The child left standing after the swap goes into the middle.

Game: Opposites
Age: 4 years+
Minimum number of participants: 2
Resources needed: Clear space.
Other Benefits: This game encourages children to think and react quickly.
Instructions: The children find a space. The teacher explains that when s/he calls out a command, for example stand up, sit down, run to your left, run to your right, walk forwards, walk backwards, touch your nose, put your hand on your head, look up, look down and so on, the children have to do the opposite. If a child doesn't do the opposite then they are out.

Game: Poison Ivy
Age: 5 years+
Minimum number of participants: 6
Resources needed: Clear space, a blindfold (optional).
Other Benefits: This game also works very well as a co-operative game. As the children are also assuming different roles – the child, the rescuer or the poison ivy – it would also work effectively as a role playing activity.
Instructions: The teacher chooses one child to be a rescuer and another child to be the person who is lost. The rest of the children are poison ivy bushes. Tell them to find somewhere to sit in the clear space and spread out. Their arms are branches which can move in the breeze, but they cannot move from their place. The child who is lost has to close their eyes or, if they want, they can be blindfolded. Tell them it is late at night and they have wandered into a forest of poison ivy. If they touch a plant or the plant touches them, they will be poisoned and will die. The rescuer has to guide the lost child from one end of the poison ivy forest to the other, but they can only use verbal instructions.

The objective of the game is for the rescuer to guide the lost child, from one end of the forest to the other, without the child being touched by the poison ivy. The lost child must listen very carefully to the instructions. If the lost child dies then another pair gets the chance to be the lost child and the rescuer.

Game: Broken Telephone
Age: 5 years+
Minimum number of participants: 4
Resources needed: Clear space.
Other Benefits: This game can be use to emphasise the importance of speaking clearly.
Instructions: Everyone sits in a circle. The teacher whispers a word or a phrase to one child. The child passes on the message to the next child in the circle. The whispering child must make sure that they are very quiet so only the child they are passing the message on to can hear them. The passing of the message is passed on around the circle, from child to child, until it reaches the last child, who calls out the message he or she received. The message at the end should be the same as the message at the beginning but that usually doesn't happen which leads to lots of laughter. The teacher can go around the circle and find out where the telephone line was broken.

Game: Pop-up Story Book
Age: 3 years+
Minimum number of participants: 2
Resources needed: Clear space, a story book.
Other Benefits: This is an excellent listening game that can be played with any number of children. It helps them to engage in the storytelling process.
Instructions: The teacher chooses a story to read that the children are familiar with. Each child is given a word. For example if the teacher was reading 'Goldilocks and the Three Bears', child A is given the word Goldilocks, child B, baby, child C, porridge, child D, bed and so on. When each child has been given a word the game can begin. All the children lie on the floor. When the child hears his/her word s/he must jump up. If they miss their turn they are out and can't pop-up anymore.

Observation Games

Good observation skills will help children to become more aware of their environment and immediate surroundings. The observation games below will help them to improve their memories and teach them to focus their attention in a more structured way.

Game: Colours
Age: 4 years+
Minimum number of participants: 2
Requirements: Clear space.
Other Benefits: This game helps the child to hone their observation skills but it can also be used as a fun warm-up or movement game.
Instructions: The teacher calls out a colour, for example blue. The children must then look for an object in the clear space that is blue. All the children must run to the blue object. The last person to get there is out.

Game: Queenie, Queenie, who has the ball?
Age: 4 years+
Minimum number of participants: 4
Resources: Clear space, a ball.
Other Benefits: This is a traditional children's game that helps with observation skills.
Instructions: A child in the group volunteers or is chosen to be the Queenie, and that child turns his/her back to everyone else. The Queenie then throws the ball over their shoulder and one of the other children catches it. They all put their hands behind their backs so that the Queenie does not know who has the ball.

The Queenie then turns around and everyone shouts:

"Queenie, Queenie who's got the ball?
Are they big, or are they small?
Are they fat, or are they thin?
Queenie, Queenie who's got the ball?"

The Queenie has to guess who has the ball through a process of elimination. If the person with the ball is the last one to be picked, that person becomes the new Queenie.

Game: What's in the bag?
Age: 3 years+
Minimum number of participants: 2
Resources: Clear space, a small bag, objects.
Other Benefits: This game stimulates the children's imagination as well as helping them to use their senses as they try to guess what's in the bag.
Instructions; The teacher puts an object into a bag. The bag goes around the circle and the children must feel it, smell it and shake it. When everyone has felt the bag, the teacher will ask each child to guess what is in the bag. When everyone has guessed, the teacher takes the object out of the bag and shows it to the children.

Game: Child Swapper
Age: 6 years+
Minimum number of participants: 6
Resources needed: Clear space.
Other Benefits: This is a difficult but enjoyable game. It also stimulates the imagination, as the Child Swapper has to think of interesting ways to make him/herself look different.
Instructions: Everyone sits in a circle and one child is chosen to be the Child Swapper. The teacher tells the Child Swapper to go out of sight and change something that is highly visible, for example change their hair, take off their socks or tie/untie their shoes. When the child is finished, have him/her walk into the middle of the circle and turn around slowly to give everyone a chance to see what has been changed. Then go around the circle while each child guesses what has been changed. The first person to guess correctly is the next child to change something about his/her appearance.

Game: Chick, Chick, Chicken
Age: 3 years+
Minimum number of participants: 5
Requirements: Clear space, a balloon.
Other Benefits: This is a very good observation game and it also promotes teamwork and co-operation.
Instructions: Show the children a balloon and tell them it is a rotten egg. Get the children to sit in a tight circle, with their hands behind their backs. One child sits in the centre of the circle and closes his/her eyes. The child in the centre of the circle is the detective. The teacher walks around the room and puts the rotten egg into one of the children's hands. The detective opens his/her eyes. The rotten egg should be passed around the circle, behind the children's backs, without the detective seeing it. The detective has three goes at guessing who has the rotten egg

Game: Does a Bear Live in the Woods?
Age: 4 years+
Minimum number of participants: 4
Resources: Clear space.
Other Benefits: This game is great for improving reaction skills.
Instructions: The teacher explains to the class that when they come across a bear in the woods they must lie down on the ground and keep very still. One child volunteers to be the bear. The bear goes to one end of the clear space and turns his/her back on the rest of the class. All the other children try to sneak up behind the bear. When the bear turns around all the children must lie very still on the ground. If the bear sees you moving s/he pulls you away to join him/her. Then there are two bears. Eventually all the children are caught moving and become bears.

Game: Kitty Wants a Corner
Age: 4 years+
Minimum number of participants: 5
Requirements: Clear space.
Other Benefits: This is a fast moving and enjoyable game that could also be used very effectively as a warm-up game.
Instructions: Get the children to spread out in a circle with one child in the middle who is the Kitty. The Kitty walks up to a child in the circle and says: "Kitty wants a corner."

The child replies: "Go and see a neighbour," and turns the Kitty away. While this is happening, the children behind the Kitty try to swap places in the circle without the Kitty seeing them. If she sees them the Kitty runs to one of the free spaces before another child reaches it. If she succeeds, the child left in the middle becomes the new Kitty. If the Kitty fails, she goes up to another child in the circle and says: "Kitty wants a corner."

Game: Magical Memories' Tray
Age: 4 years+
Minimum number of participants: 2
Resources: Clear space, ten small objects, a cloth.
Other Benefits: This game also helps with co-operation skills as the children work as a team to complete the task.
Instructions: The teacher puts ten small objects on a tray, for example a pen, a comb, a mobile phone, keys, a marker, an eraser, a ruler and so on can be used. The teacher lets the children observe the tray for two minutes and then the tray is covered with a cloth. The children must call out the objects that were on the tray.

Game: MIA – Missing in Action
Age: 4 years+
Minimum number of participants: 10
Resources needed: Clear space.
Other Benefits: This works very well as co-operative game or a warm-up game.
Instructions: Divide the class into two groups – Group A and Group B. Get Group A to look at Group B for about 30 seconds. Then Group A turn their backs on Group B. Two children in Group B quickly change places. Group A turn around and have to try to guess who has changed places. Then Group B turn their backs and Group A repeat the MIA process.

Communication Games

The games below help to develop children's non-verbal and verbal expression. Communication games improve fluency, articulation, vocal projection and language skills.

Game: Beanbag Game
Age: 4 years+
Minimum number of participants: 2
Resources: Clear space, beanbag/bags.
Other Benefits: This game can also be used as a warm-up game or a 'getting to know you' activity.
Instructions: The children stand in a circle. The teacher starts off the game by throwing a beanbag or ball to a child in the circle and asking a question at the same time, for example: "What's your name?", "Do you have a pet?", "What's your favourite colour?" and so on. The child who catches the beanbag/ball must answer the question and then throw the beanbag/ball onto the next child and asks a question. As the children get used to the game it can get faster.

Game: Granny's Knickers
Age: 5 years+
Minimum number of participants: 3
Resources needed: Clear space.
Other Benefits: This helps to improve eye contact and stimulates children's imaginations as they have to come up with unique questions.
Instructions: The children sit in a circle. One child sits in the middle of the circle and everyone in the circle takes it in turns to ask him/her a question, for example: "What did you have for breakfast?" The child in the middle is only allowed to answer "Granny's Knickers' and they must not laugh or smile. If they laugh or smile they have to change places with the child whose question made them laugh.

Game: If I could be an Animal…
Age: 3 years+
Minimum number of participants: 2
Resources needed: Clear space.
Other Benefits: This game stimulates creativity. It also helps the children to get into different roles.
Instructions: Each child in the circle takes it in turn to say for example: "Hi, my name is Julie and if I could be any animal, I would be a zebra because…"

The children should be encouraged to come up with unusual animals. They could also comment on and respond to the other children's choices of animals. At the end, the teacher could get the children to imagine that they are in the zoo and then they could walk around the clear space pretending to be their chosen animal.

Game: The Lion's Court
Age: 5 years+
Minimum number of participants: 5
Resources needed: Clear space.
Other Benefits: This engaging game works very well as a role playing activity as the children take on the roles of the different animals.
Instructions: Before starting this game it is a good idea for the teacher to talk about the different animals that are found in the jungle. The teacher should ask the children who is the King of the Jungle? The teacher then assumes the role of a lion who is the King of the Jungle. It would be a good idea to have a crown for the lion. The children can make a court for the lion with chairs and a table or with cushions. Inside the court the lion sits on a throne. Each child chooses an animal they would like to pretend to be. The lion tells the other animals he is looking for animals to join his court. One by one he calls all the animals to him and asks them why he should let them join his court. The child must say what type of animal they are and what good qualities they have and how they will be useful to the lion, the King of the Jungle.

When they have finished the King says "you may join my court" and lets them in. This is why it is a good idea to designated area in the space that represents the court. Everyone is invited to join his court and there is an animal parade at the end.

Concentration Games

The concentration games below will help children to improve their attention span. They also help children to develop their sensory awareness.

Game: I Spy (Colours and Shape)
Age: 4 years+
Minimum number of participants: 2
Resources needed: Clear space.
Other Benefits: This game is an old favourite. It can also be used to develop creativity and observation skills.
Instructions: The teacher looks around the clear space and silently selects an object that can be seen by all the children. He/she says for example: "I spy with my little eye … " and gives some description of the object, such as "something blue," "something round" or "something large." The children take turns trying to guess the object. The child who correctly guesses the selected item picks the next object.
Variation: Have all the children take turns, in a set order.

Game: Keeper of the Keys
Age: 5 years+
Minimum number of participants: 5
Resources needed: Clear space, keys and a blindfold.
Other Benefits: A very imaginative game that can be used as a warm-up or a listening game.
Instructions: The teacher chooses one child to sit in the middle of a circle, blindfolded, with keys placed close beside him/her. The child in the middle is a wicked queen. All the other children are her prisoners. The queen is blind but she has special powers. If she hears someone coming towards her, she can point at them and they turn to stone.

The teacher selects one of the prisoners to try to creep up on the queen and steal the keys without being heard. If the queen points at the prisoner, they turn to stone and another prisoner is selected by the teacher. As they creep forward, they can hide behind the prisoners who have already been turned to stone. If a prisoner successfully gets the keys before they are turned to stone, then they become the queen.

Game: Master, Master Who am I?
Age: 4 years+
Minimum number of participants: 3
Resources needed: Clear space, a blindfold.
Other Benefits: This activity also works very well as a listening game.
Instructions: All the children sit in a circle. One child is chosen to be the master. S/He must sit blindfolded in the centre of the circle. The teacher then points to one of the other children. They enter the circle and say: "Master, master, who am I?" The master must guess the child's name by listening carefully to his/her voice. If the master chooses the wrong name another child gets a chance. If s/he chooses correctly then the master swaps places with the child who entered the circle.

Game: Shopping List
Age: 4 years+
Minimum number of participants: 5
Resources needed: Clear space.
Other Benefits: This game stimulates the imagination and is very good for focussing on memory skills. It is also an excellent listening game.
Instructions: Everyone sits in a circle. The teacher starts by saying: "I went to the market and I bought an apple."

The child next to the teacher follows by saying: "I went to the market and I bought an apple and some eggs."

The next child continues by saying: "I went to the market and I bought an apple, some eggs, and a potato."

The game continues, with each child repeating what the previous children have said and adding one item to the shopping list. If a child makes a mistake then they are out of the game. The list continues until there is only one child left in the game.

Game: Follow the Leader
Age: 4 years+
Minimum number of participants: 3
Resources needed: Clear space.
Other Benefits: This game also improves reaction and observation skills.
Instructions: All the children stand in a circle and they start walking on the spot. The teacher makes a gesture and the children copy it, for example waving their left hand. Then the teacher shouts out the name of one of the children in the group and they must change or add to the action, for example waving their left and right hands.

The game can continue until everyone in the circle has had a chance to add in or to change an action.

Game: Grandma's Glasses
Age: 4 years+
Minimum number of participants: 5
Resources needed: Clear space, glasses.
Other Benefits: This is also an effective listening game.
Instructions: One child is chosen to be Grandma. Grandma puts the glasses on her head and faces a wall, at one side of the clear space. The other children in the group must go to the other side of the space. They have to try to creep up on Grandma and take her glasses. Grandma can turn around suddenly at any time. If she sees anyone moving that child must start again from the beginning.

Game: Wink Murder
Age: 4 years+
Minimum number of participants: 5
Resources needed: Clear space.
Other Benefits: This is a fun and enjoyable game that works well as an observation activity.
Instructions: The teacher chooses one child to be the murderer and another child to be the detective. No-one knows who the murderer is except for the teacher and the child who is the murderer. Everyone knows which child is the detective. All the other children sit in a circle and they must die if the murderer winks at them in an obvious way. The detective has to correctly identify the murderer. To make this game more difficult the detective has a limited number of guesses.

Game: Simon Says
Age: 3 years+
Minimum number of participants: 3
Resources needed: Clear space.
Other Benefits: This is also a very good listening or warm-up game.
Instructions: The teacher is Simon and all the children in the group stand in a line. Simon then calls out an action for the children to follow. It can be any action, e.g. 'Simon says touch your nose with your middle finger, hop on one foot or clap your hands five times and turn around. Simon, however, must say, "Simon says" before the action, otherwise the children should stand still and do nothing. If Simon doesn't say "Simon says" but just states the action by itself, such as 'stand on one leg', whoever does it is out and has to sit down. The last child left standing in the group can then be "Simon"!
Variations: Frosty Says, Superman Says, The Fairy Says, The Penguin Says, The Gingerbread Man Says and so on.

Game: Sleeping Lions/Tigers/Cows
Age: 3 years+
Minimum number of participants: 3
Resources needed: Clear space.
Other Benefits: This helps children to improve their sensory awareness.
Instructions: All the children are lions (tigers, cows or any animal they want to be). They lie down on the floor, eyes closed and stay still, as if they were sleeping. The teacher goes around the room, trying to get the lions to move. If they move, then they have to get up and help the teacher to try to get the other lions to move. They are not allowed to touch the lions, but may move close to them, tell jokes or pull faces. After five minutes, with a loud roar, tell the lions who are still on the floor to wake up.

Game: A, B, C
Age: 5 years+
Minimum number of participants: 2
Requirements: Clear space.
Other Benefits: This is also a useful listening and observation game.
Instructions: Divide the group into pairs. Child 1 and Child 2 must face each other.

They say "A, B, C." between themselves, several times. Each time one of them says "A" that child stamps their feet. When one of them says "C" they turn around. They do not do an action when either of them says B.

Child 1: "A" (Stamps feet)
Child 2: "B"

Child 1: "C" (Turn around)
Child 2: "A" (Stamps feet)

Child 1: "B"
Child 2: "C" (Turn around)

Movement Games

The games below help children to explore movement through music. They develop the children's physical skills and ensure that they can channel their energy in a fun and positive way.

The games also encourage children to use their imaginations and to be creative.

Game: Musical Hugs
Age: 3 years+
Minimum number of participants: 4
Requirements: Clear space, CD player, lively music.
Other Benefits: This is also a very useful listening and observation game.
Instructions: The children dance to lively music. When the music is stopped, the teacher shouts out a number, such as five, and the children have to get into groups of five. If the teacher calls out three then the children have to get into groups of three. Children hug each other, until the music is turned back on. They dance again, until the next time the music is stopped. The teacher calls out another number and if there are children left over, who are not in a group, they are out.

Game: Musical Statues.
Age: 3 years+
Minimum number of participants: 3
Requirements: Clear space, CD player, lively music.
Other Benefits: Promotes creativity and also helps children with role playing.
Instructions: Choose some fast music, and get the children to dance to the music and freeze when it stops.
Variation: The teacher calls out the name of an animal or object and they have to freeze into the shape of the object when the music stops.

Game: Stuck in the Mud
Age: 4 years+
Minimum number of participants: 4
Requirements: Clear space.
Other Benefits: This is also a useful observation game.
Instructions: One of the children is the catcher. All the other children have to try not to be caught. If they are caught they must stand still, with their legs apart until someone who hasn't been caught goes through their legs to free them.

This game can be timed. The catcher may only have one minute to try to catch everyone in the class.

Game: Jumping Beans
Age: 3 years+
Minimum number of participants: 2
Requirements: Clear space.
Other Benefits: This is also an effective warm-up game.
Instructions: The children should begin by walking around the room in any direction. When the teacher shouts out the following commands the children have to do the following actions.

Command	Action
Jumping Bean:	Jump up and down on the spot.
Runner Bean:	Run around the room.
Baked Bean:	Lie on the floor in a curved shape and freeze.
Jelly Bean:	Move around the room wobbling like a jelly.
Chilli Bean:	Shiver and shake.
Frozen Bean:	Children have to stand as if frozen stiff.
Long Bean:	Children put their two hands in the air and try to make themselves as long as possible.
Coffee Bean:	All cough.
Full of Beans:	Dance around really energetically.
French Bean:	Everyone says: "OOH, LA, LA!"

Game: Cat and Mouse
Age: 4 years+
Minimum number of participants: 10
Requirements: Clear space.
Other Benefits: This game can be used to improve concentration and observation skills.
Instructions: Divide all the children into pairs. In each pair, one child is a cat and the other child is a mouse. One pair is chosen to chase each other, while the rest of the pairs stand still, arms hooked together. The cat chases the mouse and when the mouse is caught the pair change roles and the mouse becomes the cat and vice versa. When the mouse wants a rest he hooks onto another pair and that pair's mouse has to run away from the original cat. If the cat is tired he hooks onto a different pair and that pair's cat chases the mouse.

Game: Double-Glazed Windows
Age: 6 years+
Minimum number of participants: 2
Resources needed: Clear space, chair.
Other Benefits: An imaginative game that is very good for promoting non-verbal communication skills.
Instructions: Divide the group into pairs. Put a chair in between child A and child B. The teacher explains that the chair represents a double-glazed window. They can see each but they aren't allowed speak to each other. The teacher gives child A a message. Child A must relay the message to child B, without making any sound or without moving their mouth. When child B guesses the message they swap and child B mimes a message for child A. Messages that usually work well include: "I love you," "Will you marry me?" "I need to use the toilet," "I'm tired," "I want to sleep," "Your house is on fire," or "Your dog made a mess in my garden."

Game: Magic Box
Age: 3 years+
Minimum number of participants: 2
Requirements: Clear space.
Other Benefits: This game stimulates children's imagination and it encourages them to be creative.
Instructions: This is a fun mime game. Everyone sits in a circle. Ask the children if they can see the box in the centre of the circle. Ask them what colour it is? What shape it is? Tell them it can be a different shape and colour, depending on where you are sitting in the circle. This is because it is a magic box.

The teacher goes into the centre of the circle first and mimes opening the box and taking out an object. She then mimes holding the object and the class must guess what it is. When the children guess correctly the teacher mimes putting it back in the box and closing it. The child who guessed correctly takes a turn at taking an object out of the box.

Game: Captain's Coming
Age: 4 years+
Minimum number of participants: 3
Resources: Clear space.
Other Benefits: This is also a very useful warm-up game.
Instructions: The teacher or a child can be chosen to be the captain. The captain calls out orders to the rest of the children, who are the crew. If a child does not follow an order correctly s/he is out!

Orders	Action
Bow:	run to the left side of the clear space.
Stern:	run to the right side of the clear space.
Port:	run to the left.
Starboard:	run to the right.
Man Overboard:	lie on your back and swim.
Submarines:	lie on your back and stick one leg straight up.
Man the Lifeboats:	find a partner, sit together, and row!
Scrub the Decks:	crouch down and pretend to clean the floor with your hands.
Climb the Rigging:	children pretend to climb a rope ladder.
Captain's Coming:	children salute and shout out, "Aye Aye Captain!"
Going Down:	on your backs, waving legs and arms in air as you drown.
Walk the Plank:	walk in a perfect straight line, one foot exactly in front of the other with arms outstretched to the sides.
Captain's Daughter:	everyone curtseys.
Hit the Deck	lie down on your stomachs.

Game: Pass the Object
Age: 4 years+
Minimum number of participants: 3
Resources needed: Clear space.
Other Benefits: This improves children's imaginations and helps them to experiment with facial expressions and body language.
Instructions; This is a follow on from the Magic Box game. The teacher mimes taking an object out of the box, for example a mouse, a rotten egg, a cream cake, chewing gum, lipstick or a puppy, and the children guess what it is. When they have guessed she passes the object around the circle. The children should react as if they were holding the actual object in their hands. Eventually the last child in the circle gets rid of the object and the teacher goes to the box and takes out a new object.

Game: Chain Mime
Age: 5 years+
Minimum number of participants: 4
Resources needed: Clear space.
Other Benefits: This is also an excellent observation game.
Instructions: Choose a child to begin the mime. They should choose a short mime of a simple action, such as making a cup of tea or cleaning their teeth. Everybody sits in a circle, with their eyes closed. The first child taps the shoulder of the child to their right and shows them the mime, once. The second child taps the child on their right and shows them the mime. Once a child has shown the mime they should keep their eyes open. Continue around the circle, until the mime has reached the last child. The last child shows the final mime to the whole class, followed by the first child showing the original mime.

Game: Yankee Doodle
Age: 3 years+
Minimum number of participants: 2
Resources needed: Clear space.
Other Benefits: This game not only helps to develop movement but also helps the children to work together in a group.
Instructions: Yankee Doodle can go to town in other ways besides riding on a pony. It can be called slideroni, skiparoni, walkaroni, hoparoni, tiptoearoni, runaroni, crawlaroni, dancearoni, for example:

> "Yankee Doodle went to town,
> Riding on a pony,
> He stuck a feather in his hat,
> And called it Skiparoni.
> Yankee Doodle skipped to town,
> Skipped to town so dandy,
> Mind the music and the step,
> And with the girls be handy."

Game: Twinkle, Twinkle Little Star
Age: 3 years+
Minimum number of participants: 2
Resources needed: Clear space, stars.
Other Benefits: This is an excellent relaxation game that can be used to close a session.
Instructions: The teacher shows the children a star. The children lie down on the floor and become a four-pointed star. They must stretch out, as hard as they can, while singing.

> "Twinkle, twinkle, little star,
> How I wonder what you are!
> Up above the world high,
> Like a diamond in the sky."

When they have finished the song, the star collapses. This can be repeated as many times as the children want.

Game: Wobbly Jelly
Age: 3 years+
Minimum number of participants: 3
Resources needed: Clear space.
Other Benefits: This is also a helpful communication game as it helps children to speak in unison and project their voices.
Instructions: The teacher helps the children learn the rhyme:

> "Two Jellies had a wobbling race,
> To see who was the wibbliest,
> Then the sun came out,
> And made them both the dribbliest."

The teacher chooses two children to be the jelly. They wobble around the room. The rest of the class is the sun and they melt them. This can be done numerous times so that all the children in the group get a chance to be the jelly.

Role Playing Games

These games are fun and imaginative and they help children to learn about the diverse roles in life. The games help children to learn how to move, speak and think differently as they become a wide variety of characters.

The activities are also an effective way to introduce young children to improvisation.

Game: Buzzy Bees
Age: 3 years+
Minimum number of participants: 2
Resources needed: Clear space, pictures of flowers.
Other Benefits: This game could also be used to promote and encourage movement.
Instructions: The teacher, who is the Queen Bee, gets the children to buzz around, with elbows flapping, searching for flowers and nectar. When they have gathered all their nectar, they fly back to the hive to feed the Queen. The children should hum as they are collecting the honey. The teacher can put pictures of flowers around the clear space.

Game: Art Gallery
Age: 6 years+
Minimum number of participants: 3
Resources needed: Clear space.
Other Benefits: This game also helps with observation and communication skills.
Instructions: The children are divided into two groups. Group A must become pictures, statues or sculptures in an art gallery. They must freeze and Group B must guess what sculptures or statues they are or what their pictures depict. When they have finished, Group B become the items in the art gallery and Group A become the visitors.

Game: Superheroes
Age: 4 years+
Minimum number of participants: 2
Resources needed: Clear space.
Other Benefits: This works well as a very effective communication activity.
Instructions: Talk about superheroes and ask the children to give you examples of some superheroes such as Batman, Spiderman, Supergirl and so on. Ask them what type of superpowers the superheroes have. Then get each child to choose a superhero and to move around the room as that superhero.

After a few minutes they all come back and form a circle. Each child shows the rest of the group how their chosen superhero moves. The rest of the group has to guess the name of their superhero and their superpower. If they have difficulty guessing then they can ask questions.

Game: The Hungry Tree
Age: 5 years+
Minimum number of participants: 3
Resources needed: Clear space.
Other Benefits: This is an excellent introduction to improvisation, as the children are free to explore their imaginations. It also helps with their co-ordination skills.
Instructions: The teacher tells the children the following story and they have to improvise the movements in the story.

The teacher gets the children to imagine they are an adventurer who wants to go on an adventure. They have to pack up their bags. The teacher asks what they need in the bags. Children's answers are usually for example water, sandwiches, sun cream, and sunglasses and so on. The children mime putting all these essentials into their bag and then mime all the actions in the adventure below.

The teacher says imagine you are walking quickly because you are so happy to be on your adventure. You see a mountain and decide you should climb it. The sun is getting hotter and hotter and you are getting tired. You get very, very tired. You wipe your brow to show how tired you are. You begin to climb slower and slower. You are very thirsty. You take out your water and have a drink. You put the bottle back in your bag and climb the rest of the way up the mountain. Eventually you get to the top. You are exhausted, very hot and very hungry. You decide it is time for your picnic. You see a lovely tree and you go and sit under its shade. You eat your picnic and go for a nap. Then suddenly you wake up and see the tree moving towards you. The tree grabs you and you realise it is a very hungry tree and wants to eat you. You scream. You struggle. You fight the branches but you are getting weaker and weaker. Then suddenly the tree stops fighting for a moment. You get your chance to escape. You quickly grab your bag, and run back down the mountain. You get to the end and you don't stop in case the hungry tree is running after you. You run all the way home, lock all the doors and hide under the table.

Game: Toy Shop
Age: 4 years+
Minimum number of participants: 4
Resources needed: Clear space.
Other Benefits: This game also promotes imagination and creative movement.
Instructions: Everyone sits in a circle and the teacher tells them to imagine that they are toys in a toy shop. They must choose which toy they want to be. Then everyone talks about what would happen if the toys came alive, how they would move and how they would sound. Each child finds a clear space and starts to move around like their toy. Next the teacher becomes the toy maker who spends all day making toys. The toys must freeze and keep very still when he is there.

Then the teacher tells them to pretend it is night when the toymaker goes to bed and all the toys come out to play. All the children move around like their toys but the toy maker hears the noise in the toyshop. The toys hear his/her footsteps and they get back into their positions and freeze. The toy maker checks to make sure the toys are alright. S/he then leaves and all the toys come out to play again.

Each time the toys hear the toymaker's footsteps they must return to their places and freeze.

Game: Wheels on the Bus
Age: 3 years+
Minimum number of participants: 2
Resources needed: Clear space, tape, coloured coins, tambourine and chairs.
Other Benefits: This is an excellent way to introduce role playing to very young children. It also encourages them to sing and move together.
Instructions: Everyone sings the song The Wheels on the Bus. Between each verse, everyone pretends to drive a bus and blow the horn. When the song is over it is a great time to "play bus" and set up rows of chairs, to look like the inside of a bus. Make a bus stop by putting some tape or a chair on the ground. Give each child several "coins" and make a small collection box. The teacher can put on a bus driver's cap and use a tambourine as a steering wheel. "Open" the bus door and invite the children on. Ask: "Where are you going?" Elicit responses such as: "To the park/to the pool/to the zoo/to the library/and so on. Say, "Two or three or four coins, please." and help the children to pay their fare.

After all the kids have boarded, start 'driving'. Sing The Wheels on the Bus together. Turn left and turn right and get the children to lean with you as you turn. Call out the stops as you go: "Next stop!"

Game: The Big, Black Cat
Age: 3 years+
Minimum number of participants: 3+
Resources needed: Clear space.
Other Benefits: The game also helps children with expressive movement.
Instructions: The teacher chooses one child to be the big, black cat. They must sleep in the corner of the clear space. The rest of the children imagine they are mice. They state to move and squeak around the room as mice. The teacher says: "The big black cat is sleeping, sleeping, sleeping; the big black cat is sleeping in the house."

Then, as children dance around the space, the teacher says: "The little mice are dancing, dancing, dancing; the little mice are dancing in the house!" Next, as the children pretend to nibble, the teacher says: "The little mice are nibbling, nibbling, nibbling; the little mice are nibbling in the house! Then as the children get into a resting position, the teacher says: "The little mice are resting, resting; resting; the little mice are resting in the house!"

The teacher continues the story and the children act it out: "The big, black cat comes creeping, creeping, creeping; the big, black cat comes creeping, creeping, creeping; and the big, black cat comes creeping in the house! The little mice go scampering, scampering, scampering, the little mice go scampering in the house! The big, black cat comes creeping in the house! The little mice go scampering, scampering, scampering; the little mice go scampering in the house! The cat chases the mice and when it catches a mouse it becomes the big, black cat.

Game: Fairy-tale Characters
Age: 5 years+
Minimum number of participants: 2
Resources needed: Clear space.
Other Benefits: This game encourages creativity and it is also an excellent movement game.
Instructions: The teacher talks to the class about fairy-tales and fairy-tale characters. Then each child must think of a fairy-tale character. One by one they go into the centre of the circle and mime part of the nursery rhyme their fairy-tale character appears in. For example they could be eating from a bowl to mime 'Little Miss Muffet', or sleeping for 'Little, Boy Blue' or sitting on a wall and falling down for 'Humpty Dumpty'.

The rest of the class tries to guess the nursery rhyme they are miming. The class can ask question but only yes and no answers are allowed.

Action Poems

Young children really like reciting poems with actions, as the actions help them to remember the words.

The poems promote co-operation, as they teach the children to speak together. They also encourage the children to use vocal expression effectively.

When Goldilocks Went to the House of the Bears

When Goldilocks went to the house of the bears,
(The children walk on the spot.)
Oh, what did her blue eyes see?
(The children point to their eyes.)
A bowl that was huge and a bowl that was small And a bowl that was tiny and that was all.
(Children make increasingly smaller shapes with their arms to represent each bowl.)
And she counted them – one, two, three!
(They use one finger to point – as if counting each bowl.)
When Goldilocks went to the house of the bears,
(Walk on the spot.)
Oh, what did her blue eyes see?
(Point to their eyes.)
A chair that was huge and a chair that was small,
And a chair that was tiny and that was all.
(Use hands to show the different heights and the size of each chair, getting smaller all the time.)
And she counted them – one, two, three!
(Use their fingers to point, as if counting each chair.)
When Goldilocks went to the house of the bears,
(Walk on the spot.)
Oh, what did her blue eyes see?
(Point to their eyes.)
A bed that was huge and a bed that was small
And a bed that was tiny and that was all.
(Use their hands to show the increasingly smaller length and size of each bed.)
And she counted them – one, two, three!
(Use their fingers to point, as if counting each bed.)
When Goldilocks went to the house of the bears.
(Walk on the spot.)
Oh, what did her blue eyes see?
(Point to their eyes.)
A bear that was huge and a bear that was small
And a bear that was tiny and that was all.
(Use hands to show the increasingly smaller height and size of each bear.)

There was a Princess Long Ago

Directions
Before you start this action poem you must choose a princess, a wicked
fairy, a prince and a horse. The chosen characters stand in the middle
of a circle with the rest of the children all around them. The stage
directions underneath each line tell the children the actions they need
to perform.

There was a princess long ago, long ago, long ago; there was a princess
long ago, long, long ago.
(Everyone curtsy/bow while the princess starts dancing.)
And she lived in a big, high tower, a big, high tower, a big, high tower;
she lived in a big, high tower, long ago, long, long ago.
*(Everyone put their hands in a triangle-shape to make a tower while the
princess keeps dancing in the middle of the circle.)*
A wicked fairy cast a spell, cast a spell, cast a spell, cast a spell. A wicked
fairy cast a spell, long ago, long, long ago.
*(The wicked fairy chases the princess inside the circle and then taps her head,
as if she is casting a spell. Everyone pretends to cast a spell, using their arms
as wands.)*
The princess slept for a hundred years, a hundred years, a hundred years,
a hundred years. The princess slept for a hundred years, a hundred years,
a hundred years, a hundred years.
*(The princess lies in the middle of the circle sleeping, while everyone else puts
their heads on their hands, as if they are also sleeping.)*
A great big forest grew around, grew around, grew around, grew around. A
great big forest grew around, grew around, grew around, grew around.
(The children cross their arms.)
A handsome prince came riding by, came riding by, came riding by, came
riding by. A handsome prince came riding by, came riding by, came riding
by, came riding by.
*(The prince runs/gallops round inside circle and everyone else gallops on the
spot.)*
He took his sword and cut the trees, cut the trees, cut the trees, cut the
trees. He took his sword and cut the trees, cut the trees, cut the trees,
cut the trees.
*(The prince moves his arms up and down inside circle and everyone else moves
their arms as if they are also cutting.)*
He woke the princess with a kiss with a kiss, with a kiss, with a kiss, with
a kiss. He woke the princess with a kiss with a kiss, with a kiss, with a
kiss, with a kiss.

(The prince gives the princess a kiss on head/cheek/lips and everyone else blows kisses.)
The wedding bells go ding, dang, ding!, ding, dang, ding!, ding, dang, ding!, ding, dang, ding! The wedding bells go ding, dang, ding!, ding, dang, ding!, ding, dang, ding!, ding, dang, ding!
(All the children use their hands to pretend to ring bells while the prince and princess dance in the middle of the circle.)
And everybody is happy now, happy now, happy now, happy now. And everybody is happy now, happy now, happy now, happy now.
(All the children smile and look happy, clapping, dancing and jumping.)

In and Out of the Dusky Bluebells

In and out of the dusky bluebells,
In and out of the dusky bluebells,
In and out of the dusky bluebells,
I am the master.

Pit-a-pat, pit-a-pat on my shoulder,
Pit-a-pat, pit-a-pat on my shoulder,
Pit-a-pat, pit-a-pat on my shoulder,
I am the master.

Directions
Everyone stands in a circle and one child is chosen to be the leader. While the first verse is being sung, the leader skips in and out around the other children in the circle. When the verse stops, the leader stands behind the closest person to him/her and pats them on the shoulder, while singing the second verse. The second child becomes the leader and they move on together. They repeat the first and second verses, patting children on the shoulder until finally all the children have become leaders.

Five Little Monkeys

Directions

Before you start, choose five monkeys, and number them from one to five, a doctor, a mother and a father. All the rest of the class can help to say the poem below.

Five little monkeys jumping on the bed,
(Five monkeys are jumping up on down on the bed.)
One fell off and bumped his head.
(Monkey One falls over and pretends to bump his head.)
Mama called the Doctor and the Doctor said:
(Mother mimes ringing the doctor.)
"No more monkeys jumping on the bed!"
(Doctor says this line by himself in an angry voice.)
Four little monkeys jumping on the bed,
(Four monkeys are jumping up on down on the bed.)
One fell off and bumped her head.
(Monkey Two falls over and pretends to bump his head.)
Papa called the Doctor and the Doctor said:
(Father mimes ringing the doctor.)
"No more monkeys jumping on the bed!"
(Doctor says this line by himself in an angry voice)
Three little monkeys jumping on the bed,
(Three monkeys are jumping up on down on the bed.)
One fell off and bumped his head.
(Monkey Three falls over and pretends to bump his head.)
Mama called the Doctor and the Doctor said:
(Mother mimes ringing the doctor.)
"No more monkeys jumping on the bed!"
(Doctor says this line by himself in angry voice.)
Two little monkeys jumping on the bed,
(Two monkeys are jumping up on down on the bed.)
One fell off and bumped her head.
(Monkey Four falls over and bumps his head.)
Papa called the Doctor and the Doctor said:
(Father mimes ringing the doctor.)
"No more monkeys jumping on the bed!"
(Doctor says this line by himself in an angry voice.)
One little monkey jumping on the bed,
(One monkey jumping up on down on the bed.)
He fell off and bumped his head.
(Monkey Five falls over and pretends to bump his head.)

Mama called the Doctor and the Doctor said:
(Mother mimes ringing the doctor.)
"Put those monkeys straight to bed!"
(Doctor says this line by himself in an angry voice.)

Five Currant Buns in a Baker's Shop

Directions
Five children can be the current buns and six children can be the customers. One child can be the baker. Everyone else can say the rhyme below

The baker lines up his currant buns in the shop. When each customer comes in to choose a currant bun, the rest of the children say the customer's name. Then the baker selects a currant bun for the customer to buy.

Five currant buns in the baker's shop,
Big and round, with a cherry on the top.
Along came .... with a penny one day,
Bought a currant bun and took it away.

Four currant buns in the baker's shop,
Big and round, with a cherry on the top.
Along came .... with a penny one day,
Bought a currant bun and took it away.

Three currant buns in the baker's shop,
Big and round, with a cherry on the top.
Along came .... with a penny one day,
Bought a currant bun and took it away.

Two currant buns in the baker's shop,
Big and round, with a cherry on the top.
Along came .... with a penny one day,
Bought a currant bun and took it away.

One currant bun in the baker's shop,
Big and round, with a cherry on the top.
Along came .... with a penny one day,
Bought a currant bun and took it away.

No currant buns in the baker's shop,
Nothing big and round, with a cherry on the top.
Along came .... with a penny one day:
"Sorry," said the baker, "no more currant buns today."

In A Dark, Dark Wood

Directions

As the children say the poem below they must all mime going into the dark woods, opening the door of the dark house, looking in the cupboard, feeling the shelf and opening the box.

Every time the poem is said the teacher can decide what is in the box, for example a ghost, a dragon, a dinosaur or a cake. The children must give the appropriate reactions to whatever the teacher, says is in the box, for example if it is a ghost they must scream whereas if it is a cake they should pretend to eat it.

"In a dark, dark wood, there was a dark, dark house.
And in that dark, dark house, there was a dark, dark room.
And in that dark, dark room, there was a dark, dark cupboard.
And in that dark, dark cupboard, there was a dark, dark shelf.
And on that dark, dark shelf, there was a dark, dark box.
And in that dark, dark box There was a .... !"

Five Little Ducks

Directions

Before you start, choose five children to be the ducks and one child to be the mother duck. Each time the verse is said by the rest of the children the ducks must waddle away quacking. When the mother duck says, "quack, quack" only the appropriate number of children must come back. Do this until there are no ducks left and then the mother duck must cry at the end.

Five little ducks,
Went out one day,
Over the hill and far away.
Mother duck said:
"Quack, quack, quack, quack."
But only four little ducks came back.

Four little ducks,
Went out one day,
Over the hill and far away.
Mother duck said:

"Quack, quack, quack, quack."
But only three little ducks came back.

Three little ducks,
Went out one day,
Over the hill and far away.
Mother duck said:
"Quack, quack, quack, quack."
But only two little ducks came back.

Two little ducks,
Went out one day,
Over the hill and far away.
Mother duck said:
"Quack, quack, quack, quack."
But only one little duck came back.

One little duck,
Went out one day,
Over the hill and far away.
Mother duck said:
"Quack, quack, quack, quack."
But none of the five little ducks came back.

Sad mother duck,
Went out one day,
Over the hill and far away.
The sad mother duck said:
"Quack, quack, quack, quack."
And all of the five little ducks came back.

Part Two: Children's Plays

The following are a selection of plays for young children all based on well-known children's stories. Each play is between five and ten minutes long. They have all been adapted to suit the various needs of the class/group.

The plays use a lot of repetition so it is very easy for young children to learn their lines. The cast list is flexible – more characters can be added and existing characters can be changed or omitted. Most of the characters can be on stage throughout the play, with children walking to the centre of the stage when it is time to say their lines.

The costumes are very simple as the children can just wear something in the colour of their animal, wear a mask or use some face paint. If the children wear a mask, make sure it isn't covering their mouths as it would make it difficult to hear them speak.

The teacher/leader can assume the role of the storyteller if the children can't read or are not at the reading level required.

The Lion and the Mouse

Characters: Three storytellers, Lion, Mouse, elephants, giraffes, snakes, owls. You can have as many elephants, giraffes, snakes and owls as you want.

(Stage Directions: all the animals are in a semi-circle on the stage, they are grouped according to their animal type. Storytellers can be placed on the right or the left of the stage.)

Storyteller 1: One hot day a lion was asleep in a cave.
(Lion is sleeping in the centre of the stage.)
Storyteller 2: Suddenly a little mouse ran over his paw.
(Mouse comes scampering out quickly and touches the Lion's paw.)
Storyteller 3: The lion woke up with a loud roar. He grabbed the mouse with his paw and said...
(Lion wakes up and grabs the mouse.)
Lion: I'm going to kill you and eat you up.
(Lion roars loudly.)
Mouse: Squeak, Squeak, Please Mr. Lion, Please don't eat me. Someday I will help you.
Lion: Ha, Ha, Ha, You, help me! Don't make me laugh but I'm not that hungry so I will let you go.
(Lion pushes the mouse away.)
Storyteller 1: The lion laughed and laughed and the mouse ran home.
Storyteller 2: A few days later the lion was out in the jungle.
Lion: I think I will scare my friends. I am very scary because I'm King of the Jungle.
(He goes to each group of animals and roars at them. All the animals are scared and move away from him.)
Storyteller 3: Suddenly the lion got caught in a trap and said...
(He is in the centre of stage when he falls to his knees.)
Lion: Oh dear how will I get out of here?
(Lion looks around the stage desperately.)
Storyteller 1: After a while he heard some elephants.
(Elephants move from the semi-circle and they circle the lion. They must make sure the audience can see their faces.)
Lion: Elephants, elephants please help me.
(Lion looks up at the elephants.)
Elephants: Oh No! We will not help you.
(Elephants trundle off back to the other animals)
Storyteller 2: Then a few giraffes passed by. He cried...
(Giraffes leave the semi-circle and move behind the lion.)

Lion: Giraffes. Giraffes please help me.
(Lion looks up at the giraffes)
Giraffes: Oh no, we will not help you.
(Giraffes go back to their place in the semi-circle.)
Storyteller 3: The lion grew cold and hungry (the lion shivers and rubs his stomach) and began to think he would never get home to his nice, warm cave. Then he heard the hissing of snakes.
(Snake moves towards the centre of the stage near the lion.)
Lion: Snake, snake, please help me. (The lion looks up at the snake.)
Snakes: Sssssssssss, oh no we will not help you, sssssssssssssssss.
(Snakes go back to the semi-circle.)
Storyteller 1: As night came the lion began to cry.
Lion: Boo hoo, I am stuck in this trap and none of my friends will help me.
Storyteller 2: Then he heard some owls hooting in the trees.
(Owls move centre stage, towards the lion.)
Lion: Owls, Owls please help me.
(Lion looks up at the owls.)
Owls: Tu Whit. Tu Whoo, owls, owls we will not help youuuuuuuuuuuu.
(Owls go back to the semi-circle.)
Storyteller 3: The lion was very sad. (Lion starts crying). He didn't know what to do. Then he heard the squeaking of a mouse.
Mouse: Squeak, squeak why are you crying Mr. Lion?
(Mouse comes from behind the other animals.)
Lion: I'm stuck in this trap and nobody will help me.
Mouse: I will help you.
Storyteller 1: The mouse began to bite through the rope and at last the lion was free.
Lion: I'm free, I'm free!! I never thought you could help me because you are too small.
Storyteller 2: From then on the lion and the mouse were very good friends.
Storyteller 3: The lesson of the story is...
Storyteller 1: ...bigger is not always better!
(Mouse and Lion hug.)

The Little Red Hen

Characters: Six storytellers, Little Red Hen, Dog 1, dogs, Cat 1, cats, Goose, geese, Duck 1, ducks (you can have as many dogs, cats, ducks and geese as you want), Farmer and Miller.

(Stage Directions: Storytellers are on the left-side of the stage and the animals are all in a semi-circle in the centre of the stage.)

Storyteller 1: Once upon a time there was a little, red hen who lived on a farm.
Storyteller 2: She was always busy!
(She moves around the stage looking busy.)
Storyteller 3: She spent all morning laying eggs for the farmer.
(Little Red Hen bends down and lays eggs. Balloons can be used for the eggs.)
Farmer: Chick Chicken! Please lay an egg for my tea.
(The Farmer come centre stage and talks to Little Red Hen.)
All Sing: *(All the animals sing)* **Chick, Chick, Chick, Chicken,**

Chick, chick, chick, chick, chicken,
Lay a little egg for me!
Chick, chick, chick, chick, chicken,
I want one for my tea!
I haven't had an egg since Easter
And now it's half past three!
So chick, chick, chick, chick, chicken
Lay a little egg for me!

Storyteller 4: After the little red hen laid her egg.
Storyteller 5: She found a grain of wheat.
Storyteller 6: She wanted to plant it in a field.
Red Hen: I think I'll ask my animal friends to help me.
(She moves towards the dogs.) Dogs, Dogs! Will you help me plant the wheat?
Dogs: Oh no, we will not help you. We are too busy burying our bones.
(They all make burying actions.)
Dog 1: Get the ducks to help you.
(They all point to the ducks.)
Red Hen: Ducks, Ducks! Will you help me plant the wheat?

(Little Red Hen moves towards the ducks)
Ducks: Oh no, we will not help you. We are too busy swimming.
(They all make swimming actions.)
Duck 1: Get the geese to help you.
(All the ducks point to the geese.)
Red Hen: Geese, Geese! Will you help me plant the wheat?
(She moves towards the geese.)
Goose: Oh no, we will not help you. We are too busy sunbathing.
(All the geese are lying on the floor enjoying the sun and rubbing lotion on themselves.)
Geese 1: Get the cats to help you.
(All geese move towards the cats.)
Red Hen: Cats, Cats! Will you help me plant the wheat?
Cats: Oh no, we will not help you. We are too busy washing our faces.
(Cats wash their faces.)
Cat 1: Plant it yourself.
Storyteller 6: No-one would help Little Red Hen so she planted it herself.
(Red Hen centre stage mimes planting the wheat.)
Storyteller 1: The sun and the rain helped the wheat to grow.
Storyteller 2: Soon the wheat was tall and yellow and needed to be cut.
Red Hen: I think I'll ask my animal friends to help me. Dogs, Dogs! Will you help me cut the wheat?
(She moves towards the dogs.)
Dogs: Oh no, we will not help you. We are too busy burying our bones.
(The dogs mime burying their bones.)
Dog 1: Get the ducks to help you.
(Dogs point at the ducks.)
Red Hen: Ducks, Ducks! Will you help me cut the wheat?
Ducks: Oh no, we will not help you. We are too busy swimming.
Duck 1: Get the geese to help you.
(All the ducks point to the geese.)
Red Hen: Geese, Geese! Will you help me cut the wheat?
Goose: Oh no, we will not help you. We are too busy sunbathing.
(The geese mime sunbathing.)
Geese 1: Get the cats to help you.
(All geese move towards the cats.)
Red Hen: Cats, Cats! Will you help me cut the wheat?
Cats: Oh no, we will not help you. We are too busy washing our faces.
(The cats mime washing their faces.)
Cat 1: Plant it yourself.

Storyteller 3: So the little, red hen cut the wheat herself.
Storyteller 4: So she took the wheat to the miller.
Storyteller 5: The miller turned the wheat into flour.
Miller: *(Gives Red Hen the bag of flour.)* Here's your flour to make bread and cakes.
Storyteller 6: The little red hen thanked the miller.
Storyteller 1: She made bread and cakes.
Red Hen: Who will help me eat the bread?
All animals: We will!
Little Red Hen: Oh no, I will eat it myself. If you want to eat the food what will you do next time?
All: We will share the work.
Storytellers: THE END

Sing Chick, Chick, Chick, Chicken.
Chick, chick, chick, chick, chicken,
Lay a little egg for me!
Chick, chick, chick, chick, chicken,
I want one for my tea!
I haven't had an egg since Easter
And now it's half past three!
So chick, chick, chick, chick, chicken
Lay a little egg for me!

The Gingerbread Man

Characters: Gingerbread Man, three storytellers, Old Woman, Old Man, Cow, Horse, Dog, Two Bears and Fox.

(Stage Directions: Three storytellers stand on the left side of the stage. Old woman is sitting on a chair – knitting or reading a book and Old Man is digging up vegetables on the right side of stage. The rest of the animals can be back stage or standing quietly in a semi-circle at the back of centre stage.)

Storyteller 1: Once upon a time, a little, old woman and a little, old man lived in a little, old house. One day, the little, old woman decided to make a gingerbread man.
Old Woman: I think I will make gingerbread for the old man's tea. He will love that.
(She gets up from the chair and goes to centre stage. She mimes making the gingerbread and putting it in the oven as Storyteller 2 speaks.)
Storyteller 2: She cut the gingerbread man out of dough. She gave him chocolate drops for eyes and a piece of lemon for his mouth. Then she put him in the oven to bake. After a while she said to herself …
Old Woman: That Gingerbread Man must be ready by now.
(Gingerbread Man comes out onto centre stage and crouches down to mime being in the oven. The Old Woman then mimes looking into the oven.)
Storyteller 3: She opened the oven door. UP jumped the gingerbread man, and away he ran, out the front door!
(Gingerbread Man jumps up and out from the oven.)
Gingerbread Man: Hello I am the Gingerbread Man.
Old Man: Don't run away. I want you for my tea.
(He puts his hand up to try and stop the Gingerbread Man.)
Gingerbread Man: Run, run, as fast as you can. You can't catch me I'm the Gingerbread Man!
Storyteller 3: The little, old woman and the little, old man ran, but they couldn't catch the gingerbread man.
(They run after him, running around the stage in a circle. Old Man and Old Woman get tired, so they stop.)
Storyteller 1: The gingerbread man ran past the cow grazing in the field.
(Cow comes out onto the stage.)
Cow: Moo! Moo! Stop! Stop! Gingerbread Man I want to eat you.
Gingerbread Man: Run, run, as fast as you can. You can't catch me I'm the Gingerbread Man!
(Cow chases him but can't catch him so she stops and goes to stage right.)

Storyteller 2: The cow ran, but she couldn't catch the Gingerbread Man. Then he met a horse drinking at the well.
(Horse comes out onto the stage.)
Horse: Neigh! Neigh! Stop! Stop! Gingerbread Man I want to eat you.
Gingerbread Man: Run, run, as fast as you can. You can't catch me I'm the Gingerbread Man!
(Horse chases him but can't catch him so he stops and goes to stage right.)
Storyteller 3: The horse ran, but she couldn't catch the Gingerbread Man. Then he met a dog playing in the field.
(Dog comes out onto the stage.)
Dog: Woof! Woof! Stop! Stop! Gingerbread Man, I want to eat you.
Gingerbread Man: Run, run, as fast as you can. You can't catch me I'm the Gingerbread Man!
(Dog chases him but he gets tired and stops and goes to stage right. Dog is panting.)
Storyteller 1: He ran between two bears having a picnic.
Two Bears: Growl! Growl! Stop! Stop! Gingerbread Man we want to eat you.
Gingerbread Man: Run, run, as fast as you can. You can't catch me I'm the Gingerbread Man!
(Bears chase Gingerbread Man but they get tired and have to stop and go to stage right.)
Storyteller 2: The bears jumped up and ran after him. They ran, and ran, but they couldn't catch that Gingerbread Man!
Storyteller 3: Soon, the Gingerbread Man came to a river and started to cry. *(Gingerbread Man cries and Fox creeps up behind him.)* He saw a fox.
Fox: Why are you crying Gingerbread Man?
Gingerbread Man: I've run away from an old woman, an old man, a cow, a horse, a dog and two picnicking bears and I can run away from you!
Fox: If you don't get across this river quickly, the old woman, the old man, the cow, the horse, the dog and the two picnicking bears, will surely catch you. Hop on my tail and I'll carry you across.
(Fox points to his tail as the old woman, the old man, the cow, the horse, the dog and the two picnicking bears start moving towards the gingerbread man.)
Storyteller 2: The Gingerbread Man saw that he had no time to lose because the old woman, the old man, the cow, the horse, the dog and the two picnicking bears were very close behind him. He quickly hopped onto the fox's tail.
(Gingerbread Man mimes getting onto Fox's tail; he holds on to his back and Fox mimes swimming.)
Fox: The water's deep, Climb up on my back so you won't get wet. OH

The water's even deeper! Climb up on my head so you won't get wet!
(Gingerbread Man holds onto Fox's back and he jumps in front. Then Fox bends down, so his head is touching Gingerbread Man's back.)
Storyteller 3: And the gingerbread man did as the fox told him.
Fox: It's too deep! Climb onto my nose so you won't get wet!
(Gingerbread Man's back touches Fox's nose.)
Storyteller 1: And the gingerbread man did that but then, with a flick of his head, the fox tossed the gingerbread man into the air and opened his mouth but the gingerbread man jumped to the other side of the river.
Gingerbread Man: (to everyone) Run, run, as fast as you can. You can't catch me I'm the Gingerbread Man!
(All the other characters are on the other side of the stage/river and they start to cry.)

The Boy who Cried Wolf

Characters: Six storytellers, six sheep, six wolves, six townspeople, a shepherd boy and his father.

(Stage Directions: the boy is sitting on a chair centre stage; the sheep are all around him grazing in the field. Townspeople and boy's father are stage left, miming working and the wolves are stage right, asleep.)

Storyteller 1: Once upon a time there was a young shepherd boy.
Storyteller 2: He lived in a lonely valley, next to a great, dark forest.
Storyteller 3: He had to look after his father's sheep and protect them from the wolves that lived in the forest.
Storyteller 4: It was a lonely job and the boy was bored.
(Boy starts to yawn and stretch.)
Storyteller 5: He wanted some fun and action.
Storyteller 6: One day...
Shepherd Boy: Oh boy! I'm so bored! There is nothing to do!
Sheep: Baa! Baa! Baa!
Sheep 1: Why are you so bored?
Sheep 2: Yes you can play with us.
Sheep 3: We always have fun following each other.
Sheep 4: Don't you like us?
Shepherd Boy: Yes, but I'm bored. I want to be in the village playing with my friends!
Sheep 5: I have an idea, if you want some excitement.
Shepherd Boy and other sheep: WHAT?
Sheep 5: Pretend there is a wolf attacking all the sheep.
Sheep 6: Don't listen to him. He (points to sheep 5) is always causing trouble.
Shepherd Boy: No, it is a brilliant plan. Let's do it right now.
(Boy goes to stage left and shouts.) Wolf! Wolf! Help! The mean, old wolf is coming.
(His father and townspeople run towards centre stage, with shotguns, sticks and shovels, as the sheep run off stage.)
Storyteller 1: His father and the townspeople came rushing to help him.
Father: Where's the wolf?
Townsperson 1: Where did he go?
Townsperson 2: I'll get him.
Townsperson 3: Did you see the wolf?
Townsperson 4: Did he go back to the forest?
Townsperson 5: Has he killed our sheep?

Shepherd Boy: False Alarm, False alarm! I thought I saw the wolf but it must have been a shadow.

Townsperson 6: False alarm, let's go home.

(Exit father and the townspeople. The sheep return, laughing. The boy sits on his chair laughing and sheep come around him)

Storyteller 2: This excitement pleased the shepherd boy.

Storyteller 3: It made him laugh and clap his hands.

(Boy laughs and claps his hands.)

Storyteller 4: A few days later, he tried the same trick again.

Storyteller 5: This time the sheep didn't know that it was a trick.

Shepherd Boy: Wolf! Wolf! The mean, old wolf is coming.

(Sheep scatter off the stage. Enter father and townspeople with shotguns, sticks and shovels.)

Father: Good lad! Tell us where the wolf is!

Townspeople: Did he go this way or that way?

Townsperson 1: He won't get far.

Townsperson 2: We could follow his tracks.

Townsperson 3: But there aren't any paw-prints.

Townsperson 4: Where's the wolf?

Shepherd Boy: False Alarm; False Alarm! I thought I saw the wolf. It must have been a shadow again.

Townspeople 5 & 6: False Alarm! Let's go home again.

(Townspeople leave and the sheep come back but this time they are relieved.)

Sheep: YOU FRIGHTENED US.

Shepherd Boy: Hee! Hee! Hee!

Storyteller 6: The boy played the trick several more times. Then one day the shepherd boy thought he saw something big and furry moving in the wood.

(Boy looks towards the wolves but shakes his head and goes to sleep with the sheep. Wolves start slinking towards the centre of the stage.)

Wolf 1: Have you seen this?

Wolf 2: What?

Wolf 3: Lots and lots of sheep.

Wolf 4: Where are they?

Wolf 5: Are you blind?

Wolf 6: Look over there!

(Points to the sheep and the boy who are all asleep.)

Wolf 4: Oh yes, now I see them.

Wolf 1: Sssh be quiet.

Wolf 2: We could have a very good dinner tonight.

Wolf 3: You mean for the rest of week.

Wolf 5: The boy is by himself.

Wolf 6: Yes no-one is there to help him. Quick let's go.

Shepherd Boy: I thought I saw something but it is only a shadow. *(Yawns)* I think I'll have another little nap.

(Wolves come to the centre stage and prowl around dramatically, gesturing to the audience to be quiet and then they grab a sheep each.)

Wolves: We are mean, old wolves with a bad reputation. It's time to eat a juicy sheep for our dinner.

Sheep: Baa! Baa! Baa!

Storyteller 1: The shepherd boy woke up!

Shepherd Boy: AHHHH. Help! Wolf! Wolf! The mean, old wolves are here!

Storyteller 2: He called and called but no-one came.

(His father and townspeople are stage left, miming working.)

Storyteller 3: They were fed up with his lies.

Storyteller 4: The wolves took all the sheep.

Storyteller 5: The moral of the story is …

Storyteller 6: … nobody believes a liar, even when they are telling the truth.

The Ants and the Grasshopper

Characters: Three storytellers, three ants, grasshopper, owls, squirrels and bears.

(Stage Directions: the owls, squirrels and bears are in a large semi-circle stage right; the storytellers are stage left and the ants are in the centre of the stage.)

Storyteller 1: One hot summer's day …
Storyteller 2: … there were some ants working hard.
Storyteller 3: They were collecting food for the winter.
(All the ants mime digging, pulling and pushing.)
Ant 1: I am so hot.
Ant 2: Me too!
Ant 3: This is very hard work.
Storyteller 1: They saw a grasshopper listening to some music on his iPod.
(Grasshopper passes by, singing and dancing; the ants stop work and look at him.)
Storyteller 2: He was dancing …
Storyteller 3: … and laughing and enjoying the lovely weather.
Grasshopper: Ants, you are so silly. You need to enjoy the sunshine.
(Ants start working again.)
Ant 1: We are working hard.
Ant 2: We want to have food for the winter.
(Grasshopper keeps dancing.)
Storyteller 1: The grasshopper continued enjoying himself.
(The Ants keep working and move stage right.)
Storyteller 2: Winter started to come and the weather got colder and colder.
Storyteller 3: The snow began to fall.
Storyteller 1: The grasshopper was cold and hungry.
(Grasshopper rubs his stomach and shivers. He looks at the owls, who start to fly around the stage.)
Grasshopper: I am cold and hungry; perhaps my friends the owls will feed me. Owls! Owls! Will you please feed me?
(Owls fly around the grasshopper and stop centre stage. They stand around the grasshopper.)
Owls: Twit Tuhooo! Oh no, we will not feed you.
(They fly back to their place in the semi-circle.)
Grasshopper: Oh dear, I know I will ask my friends the bears to feed me.
(Grasshopper walks towards the bears.) Bears! Bears! Please feed me.

(Bears are asleep so he wakes them up and they walk to the centre stage. The bears are very angry that they have been woken up.)
Bears: Growl! Growl! Oh no, we will not feed you.
(The bears go back to their place in the semi-circle.)
Storyteller 1: Then the grasshopper saw some squirrels.
(The squirrels mime eating nuts stage right.)
Grasshopper: Squirrels! Squirrels! Please feed me!
(They squirrels walk towards him.)
Squirrels: Oh no, we will not feed you.
(They hop back to stage right.)
Storyteller 2: The grasshopper was very cold and hungry. He didn't know what to do.
(Grasshopper is shivering and rubbing his stomach.)
Storyteller 3: Then he thought of the ants.
(The ants move to the centre of the stage.)
Grasshopper: Ants! Ants! Please feed me.
(The ants go into a huddle away from the grasshopper.)
Storyteller 1: The ants thought about it and decided to give him some food.
(All the ants face the grasshopper.)
Ant 1: You must promise that next year you will work hard in the summer.
(Grasshopper gets down on his hands and knees.)
Grasshopper: Oh thank you Ants, I promise.
Storyteller 1: That summer the grasshopper kept his promise and worked hard to collect food for the next winter.
(Grasshopper mimes pushing, pulling, carrying and digging with the ants.)
Storyteller 2: The lesson of the story is: fail to prepare …
Storyteller 3: …prepare to fail.

The Enormous Turnip

Characters: Three Storytellers, Old Man, Old Woman, Boy, Girl, Dog, Cat and Mouse.

(Stage Directions: storytellers on stage left and the old man in the centre. All the other characters are in a line off-stage or they can be on stage right, with each character miming doing their own thing.)

Storyteller 1: Once upon a time there lived a little old man.
Storyteller 2: One day he planted a turnip seed in his garden.
(Old man plants his seed.)
Old Man: This turnip is going to be very big and very sweet.
(Looks at the audience.)
Storyteller 3: The turnip grew and grew.
Old Man: I think it is time to dig up the turnip.
(Old man mimes trying to pull it up.)
Storyteller 1: He pulled and pulled but he couldn't pull up the turnip.
Old Man: I know, I will ask my wife to help me. Wife! Wife! Please help me to pull up the turnip.
(Wife holds on to him at the waist and they try to pull up the turnip.)
Storyteller 2: His wife came and helped him.
Storyteller 3: They pulled and pulled but they couldn't pull up the turnip.
Wife: I know, I will ask the boy to help us. Boy! Boy! Please help us to pull up the turnip.
(She calls for the boy and the boy comes to help them.)
Storyteller 1: The boy came and helped them.
(The boy holds on to her at the waist.)
Storyteller 2: They pulled and pulled but they couldn't pull up the turnip.
Boy: I know I will ask the girl to help us. Girl! Girl! Please help us to pull up the turnip.
(He calls for the girl and the girl comes to help them.)
Storyteller 3: The girl came and helped them.
(The girl holds on to him at the waist.)
Storyteller 1: They pulled and pulled but they couldn't pull up the turnip.
Girl: I know, I will ask the dog to help us. Dog! Dog! Please help us to pull up the turnip.
(She calls for the dog and the dog comes to help her.)
Storyteller 2: The dog came and helped them.
(The dog holds on to her at the waist.)

Storyteller 3: They pulled and pulled but they couldn't pull up the turnip.

Dog: I know, I will ask the cat to help us. Cat! Cat! Please help us to pull up the turnip. (He calls for the cat and the cat comes to help them.)

Storyteller 1: The cat came and helped them.

(The cat holds on to him at the waist.)

Storyteller 2: They pulled and pulled but they couldn't pull up the turnip.

Cat: I know, I will ask the mouse to help us. Mouse! Mouse! Please help us to pull up the turnip.

(She calls for the mouse and the mouse comes to help them.)

Storyteller 3: The mouse came and helped them.

(The mouse holds onto her at the waist.)

Storyteller 1: They pulled and pulled and then suddenly they pulled up the turnip.

(They all fall over.)

Storyteller 2: Everyone was very happy and they all thanked the mouse.

(Everyone shakes hands with the mouse.)

Storyteller 3: Everyone had turnip soup for dinner.

(The wife mimes giving each one of them a bowl of soup and they mime drinking it.)

Chicken Licken

Characters: Three storytellers, Chicken-Licken, Cockey-Lockey, Ducky-Lucky, Goosey-Loosey, Turkey-Lurkey and Foxy-Loxy.

(Stage Directions: Chicken Licken is moving around the centre stage, miming picking up corn. All the other animals are either off stage or on the stage miming doing different things. Storytellers are stage left.)

Storyteller 1: One summer's day, Chicken-Licken was busy picking up corn in the barnyard.
(Chicken Licken is moving around the stage, miming picking up corn.)
Storyteller 2: When all of a sudden an acorn from the big oak tree fell down and hit her right on the top of her head – kerrrr flop.
Storyteller 3: She got a terrible fright.
Chicken Licken: Oh! The sky is falling! The sky is falling! I am going to tell the king!
Storyteller 1: And away she went. To tell the king the sky is falling down. After a while she came to Cockey-Lockey.
(Cockey-Lockey walks towards Chicken-Licken who is in the centre of the stage.)
Cockey-Lockey: Where are you going Chicken-Licken?
Chicken-Licken: Oh, Cockey-Lockey. The sky is falling! I am going to tell the king.
Cockey-Lockey: I will go with you!
(They walk in a circle around the stage and they come back to the centre stage where they see Ducky-Lucky)
Storyteller 2: They went on and on and on. After a time, they met Ducky-Lucky.
Ducky-Lucky: Where are you going Chicken-Licken and Cockey-Lockey?
Chicken-Licken/Cockey-Lockey: Oh, Ducky-Lucky! The sky is falling! We are going to tell the king!
Ducky-Lucky: Wait! I will go with you.
(They walk in a circle around the stage and they come back to the centre stage where they see Goosey-Loosey.)
Storyteller 3: And they hurried off. They went on and on and on! Soon they came to Goosey-Loosey.
Goosey-Loosey: Hey, where are you two going?
Chicken/Cockey/ Ducky: Oh, Goosey-Loosey! The sky is falling! We are going to tell the king.
Goosey-Loosey: Then I will go with you!

(They walk in a circle around the stage and they come back to the centre stage where they meet Turkey-Lurkey.)

Storyteller 3: Before long they came to Turkey-Lurkey.

Turkey-Lurkey: Where are you all going in such a rush?

All: Oh, Turkey-Lurkey. The sky is falling! We are going to tell the king.

Turkey-Lurkey: Well, hey, wait for me! I will go with you.

(They walk in a circle around the stage and they come back to the centre stage where they see the fox)

Storyteller 1: They went on and on and on. After a while they came to Foxy-Loxy.

Foxy-Loxy: Say, where are you all going?

All: Foxy-Loxy! Foxy-Loxy! The sky is falling! We are going to tell the king.

Foxy-Loxy: Well, I know a short cut to the king's palace. Follow me.

Turkey: Oh, great! He knows a short cut to the king's palace!

Storytellers: They went on and on and on. Then they came to Foxy-Loxy's house.

(They all follow Foxy-Loxy, walking in a straight line.)

Foxy: This is the short cut to the palace. I'll go in first and then you follow me, one-by-one.

(One-by-one they go into the den. The den can be off-stage in the front or behind stage.)

Storytellers: In went Turkey-Lurkey. Sssssnap! Off went Turkey-Lurkey's head. In went Goosey-Loosey. Kerrrr-POP! Off went Goosey-Loosey's head. In went Ducky-Lucky. Kerrrr-unch! Off went Ducky-Lucky's head. In went Cocky-Lockey.

(Chicken-Licken looks into the den and sees what is happening.)

Cockey-Lockey: (Excitedly) Go Home, Chicken-Licken! Go Home!

Storyteller 1: Can you guess what happened next? (pause) Kerrrrr-Aaaack! Off went Cockey-Lockey's head.

Storyteller 2: Chicken-Licken ran home. (Chicken-Licken runs really fast around the stage, looking scared) She did not tell the king that the sky was falling.

Storyteller 3: And since that day the others have never been seen again. And the poor king has never been told that the sky is falling down!

Rhyming Plays

The following are a collection of five rhyming plays or poems. They can be used in a variety of ways:

- o The leader could read them and get all the children to act out or mime the different parts for fun or in front of an audience.
- o They could also be recited. Each child could learn four lines each and they could recite it as a choral piece.

These plays help children with their vocal expression and give them an understanding of rhythm.

The Lion and the Mouse

There was a lion who lived in a cave.
He was extremely big and terribly brave.
The lion was not frightened of anything
Because he was the fearsome jungle king.

One day he was asleep near his house
When he was woken by a little mouse.
The lion grabbed the mouse with his large paw
He licked his lips and opened his wide jaw.-

The little mouse looked at him with sheer dread -
He didn't want to be some scrumptious spread. -
"Squeak, squeak, Mr. Lion do not eat me
Some day I will help you so let me be."

"You help me," he said "I don't think so
But I'm not that hungry, so off you go."
One day while hunting deep in the jungle
The lion tripped over and took a tumble.

Suddenly he was stuck in an evil trap
The other animals began to clap.
He saw some grey elephants and he cried:
"Elephants, please help me I've swallowed my pride."

"Oh Mr. Lion we will not help you
So how does it feel to be in a stew?"
The elephants said with extreme delight
And off they trundled into the dark night.

The lion waited and a few hours passed
Then out of the blue he saw some giraffes
"Giraffes, Giraffes," he said, "please, please help me."
The Giraffes looked at him and decided to flee.

He was extremely hungry and very cold
He was terribly tired and feeling less bold.
When all of a sudden down by the lake
He heard the hissing of a slimy snake.

"Snake, please, please help me I'm stuck in a trap,

I feel confused and I'm all in a flap."
The snake hissed: "Jungle King I must admit,
You really do look like a proper twit."

Snake laughed and laughed and felt real good
And away he slithered into the deep wood.
The Lion felt a sense of despair,
He was stuck outside in the cold night air.

Then all of a sudden out from his house
Came the patter of the little brown mouse.
"Pardon Lion I'm not one for prying
But please tell me why you are crying?"

The lion told the mouse his whole story
In all its wondrous gruesome glory.
The little mouse began to gnaw and gnaw
The scary lion sat there full of great awe.

At last, the lion roared: "I'm FREE; I'm FREE."
With that he invited the mouse home for tea.

The Gingerbread Man

One day an old woman wanted to treat
Her hungry old husband who loved to eat.
She decided to bake in her large pan
Ingredients for a gingerbread man.

She mixed some flour and some sugar with eggs,
She gave him a nose, two eyes and two legs.
Then she popped him in the hot oven to bake
She was looking forward to eating cake.

The gingerbread man bellowed: "Let me out!"
The little old woman heard his loud shout.
She ran to the oven and she opened the door.
The gingerbread man jumped onto the floor.

He stood silently in complete surprise.
Then he yawned and stared and stretched his eyes.
He decided to run out the back door.
"Stop! Stop!" cried the old man with a loud roar.

He ran and ran until he met a cow
Who said: "I'm feeling rather peckish now."
"Run, run, run," he said "as fast as you can
You can't catch me I'm the Gingerbread Man."

He passed a horse who looked awfully posh.
He was very hungry and looking for nosh.
"Run run, run," he said, "as fast as you can
You can't catch me I'm the Gingerbread Man."

He ran and ran until he came to a lamb
Who said: "Mmmm you will taste good with some jam."
"Run run, run," he said, "as fast as you can
You can't catch me I'm the Gingerbread Man."

He came to the river and gave a cry
"I cannot cross this so I won't even try."
The fox crept up and said with a quiver:
"Hello, would you like to cross this river?"

The Gingerbread Man jumped on the fox's back
He was feeling happy and quite relaxed.
"Oh," said the fox, "I am so glad we met
But jump on my nose so you won't get wet."

The end of the story you already know,
Even though it happened a long time ago
That cunning, old fox had his massive feast
And then off he strolled towards the Far East.

The Enormous Turnip

A long, long time ago,
There was a man who liked things to grow.
One day he planted a turnip seed,
To help his family who he had to feed.

The turnip seed grew and grew
Until it was the size of Peru.
The turnip became so very big.
It was no longer the size of a twig.

The man decided to pull it up
But the turnip appeared to be in a strop.
The man pulled and pulled until he gave a yelp.
He knew it was time to call for help.

"Come come," he called to his wife.
"Please help me I'm in some strife."
The wife replied with a knowing grin:
"Oh dear me, look at the pickle that you are in."

They pulled and pulled until they could pull no more.
Their legs and arms were extremely sore.
The wife decided to call for the boy:
"Please help," she said, "we have no joy."

They pulled and pulled until they could pull no more.
The boy thought to himself: "Oh what a bore!"
The boy decided to call for the girl:
"Please help us," he said, "just give it a whirl."

They pulled and pulled until they could pull no more.
The girl stumbled and they all fell on the floor.
The girl decided to call for the dog:
"Please help us," she said, "we are missing a cog."

They pulled and pulled until they could pull no more.
The dog said to the others: "What's all this for?"
The dog decided to call for the cat:
"Please help us," she said, "the turnip is so very fat!"

They pulled and pulled until they could pull no more.
The cat was tired so he began to snore.
The cat decided to call for the mouse:
"Please help us," she said, "come on out of your house."

They pulled and pulled and pulled and pulled

When

Suddenly

POP

Out from the ground the turnip went **PLOP!**
They looked at the turnip and knew they were onto a winner
They were all so pleased they went home and had dinner.

The Trial of the Big, Bad Wolf

The Wolf took the stand in his own defence
His sense of shock was truly immense.
He was accused of the most dreadful crime
And it looked like he would do some real time.

It all began deep in the dark forest.
He saw a girl that looked like a florist.
She had some food that looked real good.
She told him her name was Red Riding Hood.

She was off to see her Gran who was sick.
She couldn't stop as she had to be quick.
"How very rude not to stop," Wolf said
"How silly she is with a name like Red."

He thought to himself: "Mmmmm I will play a trick.
He ran to Granny's and boy was he quick.
Gran was asleep but she suddenly awoke.
He explained and soon she was in on the joke

Then there came a great, loud knock at the door.
Granny ran fast and hid under the floor.
The wolf dressed up and jumped into the bed.
He said: "Oh please come in my sweet, Little Red."

Little, Red Riding Hood entered the house
She tip-toed and whispered and was quiet as a mouse.
She looked at her gran and got a surprise
"Oh Granny," she said, "you have very big eyes."

Red sat on the bed and moved in close
She was very confused but then she froze:
"You aren't Granny!" and she screamed for help.
"Oh please calm down," the wolf said with a yelp.

Suddenly in from the forest came the woodcutter
"To be honest," Wolf said, "he looked like a nutter."
He grabbed the wolf by his neck and declared:
"Tell me where Granny is or you will be scared."

"If you don't tell me now I will give you what for!"
The wolf shouted loudly: "She is under the floor."
Granny came out, looking shocked and confused
She seemed befuddled, upset and bemused.

"Please Gran explain you were in on the joke."
"Oh no," she cried and collapsed with a stroke.
"That's the true story," Wolf said with a plea.
But the jury replied guilty and smiled with glee.

Three Billy Goats Gruff

Once upon a time on the side of a hill,
There lived three goats gruff who were all called Bill.
They decided to travel across the bridge,
To eat some green grass on a nearby ridge.

The trouble was for the Billy Goats Gruff
Crossing the big bridge was extremely tough.
Because under the bridge there lived a fierce troll
Who was often seen about on patrol.

One hot day the youngest Billy Goats Gruff
Decided, that's it, he had just had enough.
Clippety, Clippety, Clippety, Clop.
He crossed the bridge with a skip and a hop.

From under the bridge out came the large troll.
His heart was black and his eyes were like coal.
His very sharp fangs were terribly scary
And his body was incredibly hairy.

"Who is that crossing my big bridge?" he said.
He looked very angry and his face was red.
"Oh kind Mr Troll, please, please let me pass
I am only going to eat some sweet grass."

"Look at me, I'm too small for you to eat
Wait for my brother he has got more meat."
The troll looked and said: "Alright, off you go
I suppose I can wait for you to grow."

One hot day the middle Billy Goats Gruff
Decided to cross the bridge in a huff.
Clippety, Clippety, Clippety, Clop.
He crossed the bridge with a skip and a hop.

Out from the bridge, from the cold dead of night
Came the ugly fierce troll with sheer delight
"Who is that crossing my bridge?" he growled.
His eyes were glowing and his forehead scowled.

"Oh please, don't eat me," the middle goat replied.
"All I want is to get to the other side.
Please, please, let me go," he said with vigour.
"Do you not know my brother is bigger?"

The nasty troll agreed that time he could bide
And off middle goat skipped, to the other side.
One hot day the biggest Billy Goats Gruff
Crossed the big bridge as he was feeling tough.

Clippety, Clippety, Clippety, Clop
He crossed the bridge with a skip and a hop.
From under the bridge the fierce troll jumped out
He gave a big scream and even louder shout.

"Finally I am on to a winner
I'm going to eat you for my DINNER."
The biggest Billy Goat Gruff stood and stared
His nostrils suddenly began to flare.

He tossed the troll right into the stream
The troll was frightened and gave a loud scream.
The goat trotted in triumph over the bridge
And joined his brothers on the green, grassy ridge.

Part Three: Monologues for Children

The following section is a selection of monologues for young children. The monologues can be used for drama examinations, competitions, performances or they can just be done for fun.

The monologues also help the children to get into different roles and to use their imagination. In addition they stimulate children's creativity.

Monologues for Children (Girls)

Cinderella
(Cinderella is walking around the room, dusting the furniture.)

Cinderella: I am so tired I can hardly keep my eyes open. I'll never get all this dusting and polishing done before they come home from the ball. I wonder if I could ask some of my animal friends to help me. But they have all gone to sleep for the night.

(Softly) Puss... puss... puss.... Wake up and help me and I'll give you a nice saucer of milk. Oh dear, he's too sleepy. I wonder if they are all having a nice time at the ball.

(Sits down) I wish I was there. I'll just sit down for a moment and imagine I am there too. *(Falls asleep)*

Sleeping Beauty
(Picks up letters from the ground, looks at them and throws them back down again.)

Bad Fairy: Bills! Bills! Bills! No invitation here for me. The king and queen must have forgotten all about me. How could they do such a thing? I bet all the other fairies have their invitation to the princess's Christening. But they are all goody-two shoes.

(In a funny voice) "Yes King! No King! Three bags full King! Oh please invite us to your daughter's Christening King." I will get them back for this. How dare they! How very dare they?

(Softly) I wonder ... mmmmmmmmm ... I know what I will do. Since all the other fairies will give her gifts. I will too. Now where is my book of magic?
(Gets her book and opens the page.)

Oh yes, here it is! I wish ... I wish ... that on her 21st birthday the princess will prick her finger and die.

Ha! Ha! Ha!

Snow White

Snow White: *(Puts on her shawl)* What a lovely, sunny day it is today. I think I'll walk down to the shops and get something nice for the dwarves' dinner. I wonder what they would like. Perhaps a nice, juicy hamburger and I'll dig up some potatoes and make a big bowl of chips.

(Picks up comb) Oh! Look I'll wear that pretty comb in my hair that the old lady gave me. Oh dear I feel so dizzy I think I'll sit down for a minute.

(Sits down with head her hands.)

The Elves and the Shoemakers

(Old woman is sitting at a table, reading her horoscope and drinking a cup of very weak tea.)

Old Woman: This tea is so weak it tastes just like water. I suppose I must have used that teabag at least six times by now. (Sighs) I wonder if there is any good fortune in store for me. Now let me see. (Looking through the paper, mimes reading) Leo – um - 'Good luck and riches are coming your way shortly.' What rubbish they write. (Throws down the paper.) We don't even have enough money to buy leather to make one pair of shoes. Soon we won't have a roof over our heads. I think I'll just go down to the butcher and see if he will give me a bone to make some soup for our dinner.

(She gets up and goes to a chair where her old shawl and coat are lying. When she picks it up she discovers the most beautiful pair of shoes underneath it.)

Oh my goodness! Oh my goodness! Where did they come from? They are the most beautiful shoes ever made. Why if we sell these we can buy food and enough leather to make at least two pairs of shoes.

(Takes the shoes in her hands and strokes them.) 'Good luck and riches are coming your way.' Perhaps it is true after all.

Beauty and the Beast

Beauty: I don't know how I am going to tell you this dear Beast. I had an email from my sister Anne, she writes that my father is very ill and wants me to come home to see him. I have been away such a long time now. I am sorry Beast but I will have to leave you for a little while. Now don't cry. I will come back. Look, I will give you this as a promise that I will return.

(Takes a ring from her finger and gives it to him.)

Take this. It is my pledge that I will be with you again as soon as my father is better.

Red Riding Hood

(Enters skipping and then stops when she sees the wolf.)

Red Riding Hood: Hello Mr. Wolf. Isn't it a lovely day? I am just taking some food and flowers to my granny's cottage. Do you like the flowers? Just smell them; they are so nice. I bet you prefer food don't you.

(Puts down her basket and offers him some food.)

Look at that poor woodcutter over there I wonder should I give him some food. Oh, he has his own lunch. Anyway I think he is phoning someone. Goodness why are you running off in such a hurry? Was it something I said? Mr. Wolf, Mr. Wolf, please come back.

Monologues for Children (Boys)

Jack and the Beanstalk

(Sneaks downstairs on his tip-toes, takes milk and bread out of fridge and sits down.)

Jack: I have just come downstairs for a nice glass of milk and a cheese sandwich. (Pours the milk) I was sent to bed without any supper because my mother was very angry at me. You see we are very poor and we had to sell our cow Daisy. I went to the market to sell Daisy but I met an old man on the way who told me that he would give me three magic beans in return for the cow. My mother was very angry when I showed her the magic beans. She threw them out the window.

(Goes to the door and opens it) I wonder if I can find them.

(Looks up to the sky) Oh my goodness the beans have grown into a massive beanstalk and it is going way up into the sky. I wonder … if I could climb it.

Red Riding Hood

Woodcutter: I don't like the look of that wolf. He is out there in the woods jumping about and hiding behind trees. I don't think he is up to any good.

(Sits down and takes out his sandwiches from his pocket.)

Ah, these look good. My wife makes a very tasty sandwich. Now where is that fellow gone again? Oh he is over there talking to the little girl in the red shawl. I think I'll just call the police to come and keep on eye on him.

(Takes out phone.)

Gingerbread Man

(Runs to the edge of the river.)

Gingerbread Man: Oh my goodness, what am I going to do now? If I don't get across the river I will surely get caught.

(He starts to cry but hears a noise and looks up.)

Oh you gave me fright. I didn't see you there, Mr. Fox. I am upset because I have run away from an old man, an old woman, a horse, a cow and a dog because they all want to eat me. I don't know what to do because I can't swim. Do you think you can help me? If I jump on your back you can carry me across and then I will be free. Oh thank you, thank you, Mr. Fox.

(He climbs onto the fox's back) Oh Mr. Fox I am getting wet. I will climb onto your head. Oh my I am getting wetter I will climb onto your nose. Ahhhhhhhhhhhhhhhhhhhhhhhhhhh

Dick Whittington

(Sitting in a chair with his head in his hands, he looks up and talks to his cat.)

Dick: I had such a strange dream last night, Puss. I heard a voice telling me that I was to go out and seek my fortune and that one day I would become Lord Mayor of London. What should I do, Puss? If we remain here we will starve. There is nothing left to eat in the house just some old scraps.

(Pours out a saucer of milk.)

Look this is your last saucer of milk. But it is such a long walk to London. You are such a clever cat; tell me what we should do.

(He listens to the cat's reply.)

Okay we'll go. It will be such a big adventure. We'll pack up everything we have in this old bag; apples and bread for me and some meat for both of us. Come on Puss, best foot forward. We'll never set foot in this place again and if I make my fortune I'll buy you a little gold bell to wear around your neck and a silken cushion for you to sleep on at night.

Beauty and the Beast

(Sitting down, looking at a picture of Beauty.)

Beast: I am so ugly I don't know how you can bear to be near me. You are the only one who has been kind to me. I never had a friend before in the entire world. When I was young none of the children would play with me. I had to stand alone in the playground and all the other children ran around. They played football and chasing but they wouldn't let me join in. They said I was too big and they were frightened of me. If you go away (wipes his eyes) I think I shall die, I shall be so lonely.

Made in the USA
Columbia, SC
02 April 2018